UNDERSTANDING DRUGS

Ecstasy

TITLES IN THE *UNDERSTANDING DRUGS* SERIES

UNDERSTANDING DRUGS

Ecstasy

M. FOSTER OLIVE, Ph.D.

CONSULTING EDITOR
DAVID J. TRIGGLE, Ph.D.
University Professor
School of Pharmacy and Pharmaceutical Sciences
State University of New York at Buffalo

CHELSEA HOUSE
PUBLISHERS
An imprint of Infobase Publishing

Chelsea House
An imprint of Infobase Publishing
132 West 31st Street
New York NY 10001

Library of Congress Cataloging-in-Publication Data

Olive, M. Foster.
  Ecstasy / M. Foster Olive ; consulting editor, David J. Triggle.
    p. cm. — (Understanding drugs)
  Includes bibliographical references and index.
  ISBN 978-1-60413-538-1 (hardcover : alk. paper) 1. Ecstasy (Drug) I. Triggle, D. J. II. Title. III. Series.

  RM666.M35O45 2009
  615'.7883—dc22

                    2010005458

Chelsea House books are available at special discounts when purchased in bulk quantities for businesses, associations, institutions, or sales promotions. Please call our Special Sales Department in New York at (212) 967-8800 or (800) 322-8755.

You can find Chelsea House on the World Wide Web at
http://www.chelseahouse.com

Text design and composition by Kerry Casey
Cover design by Alicia Post
Cover printed by Bang Printing, Brainerd, MN
Book printed and bound by Bang Printing, Brainerd, MN
Date printed: September 2010
Printed in the United States of America

10 9 8 7 6 5 4 3 2 1

Contents

Foreword

THE USE AND ABUSE OF DRUGS

For thousands of years, humans have used a variety of sources with which to cure their ills, cast out devils, promote their well-being, relieve their misery, and control their fertility. Until the beginning of the twentieth century, the agents used were all of natural origin, including many derived from plants as well as elements such as antimony, sulfur, mercury, and arsenic. The six-teenth-century alchemist and physician Paracelsus used mercury and arsenic in his treatment of syphilis, worms, and other diseases that were common at that time; his cure rates, however, remain unknown. Many drugs used today have their origins in natural products. Antimony derivatives, for example, are used in the treatment of the nasty tropical disease leishmaniasis. These plant-derived products represent molecules that have been "forged in the crucible of evolution" and continue to supply the scientist with molecular scaffolds for new drug development.

Our story of modern drug discovery may be considered to start with the German physician and scientist Paul Ehrlich, often called the father of che-motherapy. Born in 1854, Ehrlich became interested in the ways in which synthetic dyes, then becoming a major product of the German fine chemi-cal industry, could selectively stain certain tissues and components of cells. He reasoned that such dyes might form the basis for drugs that could inter-act selectively with diseased or foreign cells and organisms. One of Ehrlich's early successes was development of the arsenical "606"—patented under the name *Salvarsan*—as a treatment for syphilis. Ehrlich's goal was to create a "magic bullet," a drug that would target only the diseased cell or the invad-ing disease-causing organism and have no effect on healthy cells and tissues. In this he was not successful, but his great research did lay the groundwork for the successes of the twentieth century, including the discovery of the sul-fonamides and the antibiotic penicillin. The latter agent saved countless lives during World War II. Ehrlich, like many scientists, was an optimist. On the eve of World War I, he wrote, "Now that the liability to, and danger of, disease are to a large extent circumscribed—the efforts of chemotherapeutics are directed as far as possible to fill up the gaps left in this ring." As we shall see in the pages of this volume, it is neither the first nor the last time that science has proclaimed its victory over nature, only to have to see this optimism dashed in the light of some freshly emerging infection.

From these advances, however, has come the vast array of drugs that are available to the modern physician. We are increasingly close to Ehrlich's magic bullet: Drugs can now target very specific molecular defects in a number of cancers, and doctors today have the ability to investigate the human genome to more effectively match the drug and the patient. In the next one to two decades, it is almost certain that the cost of "reading" an individual genome will be sufficiently cheap that, at least in the developed world, such personalized medicines will become the norm. The development of such drugs, however, is extremely costly and raises significant social issues, including equity in the delivery of medical treatment.

The twenty-first century will continue to produce major advances in medicines and medicine delivery. Nature is, however, a resilient foe. Diseases and organisms develop resistance to existing drugs, and new drugs must constantly be developed. (This is particularly true for anti-infective and anticancer agents.) Additionally, new and more lethal forms of existing infectious diseases can develop rapidly. With the ease of global travel, these can spread from Timbuktu to Toledo in less than 24 hours and become pandemics. Hence the current concerns with avian flu. Also, diseases that have previously been dormant or geographically circumscribed may suddenly break out worldwide. (Imagine, for example, a worldwide pandemic of Ebola disease, with public health agencies totally overwhelmed.) Finally, there are serious concerns regarding the possibility of man-made epidemics occurring through the deliberate or accidental spread of disease agents—including manufactured agents, such as smallpox with enhanced lethality. It is therefore imperative that the search for new medicines continue.

All of us at some time in our life will take a medicine, even if it is only aspirin for a headache or to reduce cosmetic defects. For some individuals, drug use will be constant throughout life. As we age, we will likely be exposed to a variety of medications—from childhood vaccines to drugs to relieve pain caused by a terminal disease. It is not easy to get accurate and understandable information about the drugs that we consume to treat diseases and disorders. There are, of course, highly specialized volumes aimed at medical or scientific professionals. These, however, demand a sophisticated knowledge base and experience to be comprehended. Advertising on television is widely available but provides only fleeting information, usually about only a single drug and designed to market rather than inform. The intent of this series of books, **Understanding Drugs**, is to provide the lay reader with intelligent, readable, and accurate descriptions of drugs, why and how they are used, their limitations, their side effects and their future. The series will discuss both *"treatment drugs"*—typically, but not exclusively, prescription drugs, that have well-established criteria of both efficacy and safety—and *"drugs of abuse"* that have pronounced pharmacological and physiological effects but that are considered, for a variety of reasons, not to be considered for therapeutic purposes. It is our hope that these books will provide readers with sufficient information to satisfy their immediate needs and to serve as an adequate base for further investigation and for asking intelligent questions of health care providers.

—David J. Triggle, Ph.D.
University Professor
School of Pharmacy and Pharmaceutical Sciences
State University of New York at Buffalo

1
Overview of Ecstasy

Karen had only used Ecstasy once in her life. It was just after college and she was with a group of friends going to a Crosby, Stills, and Nash concert. It was being held at an outdoor amphitheater during the end of the summer with gorgeous weather and a slight breeze. An hour or so after taking an Ecstasy tablet, it slowly started to take effect, and Karen remembered feeling as if the music notes were starting to blow in her hair and not the wind. She felt like she could really feel the music all over herself, and the lights from the concert looked much brighter. Although feeling calm and peaceful, it was hard for Karen to sit still. At one point she decided that she needed to leave the main concert area and go for a walk with her friend Kristi. Since Karen loved nature, she felt the urge to be out among the trees, so she and Kristi ventured into a nearby wooded area outside the concert venue. Karen felt that all her senses were heightened—especially her senses of touch, smell, and taste. The leaves of the trees looked greener, the feel of the tree bark on her hands felt so soft, and everything felt more pronounced in a positive way. After the concert, Karen and her friends went to a small nearby cozy bar and started to write poetry on paper napkins. Even the napkins felt extremely soft to the touch. As she wrote on the napkins, she felt the words pour out of her mind, as if she were a master poet. The next day Karen woke up feeling tired and drained.

WHAT IS ECSTASY?

Ecstasy is the common name for 3,4-N-methylenedioxy-N-methylamphet-amine (often abbreviated **MDMA**), a drug that is very popular among teen-agers and young adults. Ecstasy is currently illegal in the United States and many other countries, and is classified by the U.S. Drug Enforcement Ad-ministration (DEA) as a Schedule I Controlled Substance, which means it carries a high probability of addiction and has no accepted medical value (see Appendix for a more detailed description of how the DEA classifies other controlled substances). Ecstasy is often used at **rave** parties (social gatherings of young people with loud dance music, flashing or moving lights, and use of alcohol and other drugs), as well as indoor dance clubs (and is thus often referred to as a **club drug**). Ecstasy is usually taken orally in the form of a pill or tablet, which is often imprinted with some form of symbol or icon.

A Hallucinogen

A **hallucination** is either something that a person senses (i.e., hears, sees, smells, feels, or tastes) that does not really exist, or is a distortion of the per-ception of a normal object or person. Visualizing a television growing legs and transforming into a gigantic tarantula, or watching the moving beams of light reflecting off of a mirrored "disco" ball transform into a swirling gal-axy of millions of colors are examples of hallucinations. Hallucinations are commonly experienced by people who suffer from mental disorders such as schizophrenia; in people with this disorder, however, the hallucinations are most often hearing voices. Hallucinations are often frightening and disturb-ing to many people who experience them, but some find hallucinations to be enjoyable, tantalizing, and stimulating.

A chemical substance that produces hallucinations is called a **hallucino-gen** (in other words, it "generates hallucinations"). Sometimes hallucinogens are referred to as **psychedelic** drugs or **psychedelics**. The most widely used hallucinogens are lysergic acid diethylamide (LSD); phencyclidine (PCP); ketamine (often nicknamed "Special K"); psilocybin (the main hallucinogen-ic chemical found in certain types of wild mushrooms, often called "magic mushrooms" or "shrooms"); mescaline (the main hallucinogenic chemical found in the Peyote cactus); and other natural or synthetic chemicals such as

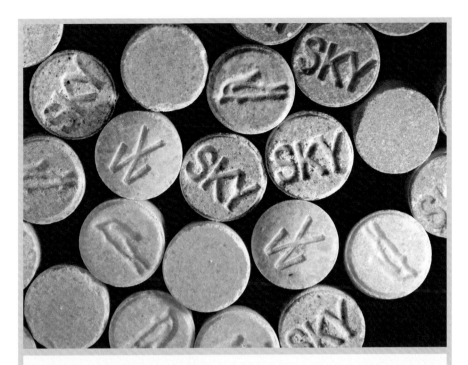

Figure 1.1 Ecstasy tablets come in many shapes and sizes, like the ones shown here. The tablets may be stamped with a variety of shapes, letters, and logos, which often make them appealing to young and unsuspecting users. (*Drug Enforcement Administration*)

dimethyltryptamine (DMT); 5-methoxy-diisopropyltryptamine (commonly referred to as "Foxy"); 4-bromo-2,5-dimethoxyphenethylamine (frequently referred to as 2C-B); and Salvia divinorum (a hallucinogenic plant commonly referred to as "Salvia"). Some of these hallucinogens have been used in religious ceremonies by various cultures around the world for centuries, but the use of hallucinogens for recreational purposes in the United States did not become popular until the cultural revolution of the 1960s. The use of hallucinogens continues today, especially among teenagers and young adults.

When compared to hallucinogens like LSD, PCP, and ketamine, which can produce vivid and often frightening hallucinations, the hallucinogenic effects of Ecstasy are relatively mild to moderate. Low to moderate doses of Ecstasy intensify the senses of touch, sound, taste, and vision. By taking Ecstasy at a crowded rave party with colored flashing lights, music, and close contact with other people, a person's experience under the influence of this drug is more intense and pleasurable than if the person were alone. Higher doses of Ecstasy, however, can produce more unpleasant effects, such as depression, panic, frightening hallucinations, confusion, and anxiety.

An Empathogen and Entactogen

In addition to the intensification of the perception by the senses and some mild to moderate hallucinatory effects, some of the other psychological effects of Ecstasy are (1) an ability to make the user experience extreme feelings of pleasure, euphoria, confidence, and high self-esteem (hence the name "Ecstasy"), (2) an ability to produce feelings of love, closeness, communication, and peace toward others, (3) an ability to experience and understand the emotions and feelings of other people (**empathy**), and (4) an ability to increase positive feelings about oneself and the world within he or she lives

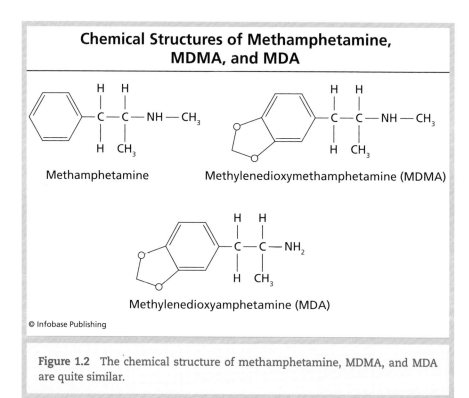

Figure 1.2 The chemical structure of methamphetamine, MDMA, and MDA are quite similar.

(known as **entactogenesis**).[1] Thus, Ecstasy is commonly referred to as an **empathogen** or an **entactogen**.

A Stimulant

The chemical structure of Ecstasy is similar to that of the highly addictive drug methamphetamine. As such, it also shares some of the same biological effects of methamphetamine, including increases in heart rate (**tachycardia**), blood pressure (**hypertension**), body temperature (**hyperthermia**), and physical and emotional energy and alertness. Ecstasy is therefore considered both a stimulant and a hallucinogen.

ECSTASY DOSES AND IMPURITIES

Ecstasy is synthesized illegally in laboratories, primarily in Europe, and then smuggled to numerous other countries around the globe. In the United States, each Ecstasy tablet typically costs $25 or more. Because the drug is made illegally, there is no regulated quality control to ensure that a precise amount of MDMA is present in each tablet. Herein lies one of the key problems of Ecstasy use. The typical dose of Ecstasy that users find enjoyable is in the range of 50 to 150 milligrams, and additional tablets can be taken as "boosters" to prolong the effects. However, a tablet of Ecstasy can contain anywhere from 50 to 300 milligrams of MDMA.[2] So, if a particular batch of Ecstasy tablets contains lower amounts (i.e., 50 milligrams per tablet) of MDMA, a single tablet may be insufficient to produce the desired effects, so the user may take several pills (i.e., "double stacking" or "triple stacking"). On the other hand, if a particular batch of Ecstasy tablets contains high amounts of MDMA (i.e., 300 milligrams per tablet), a single tablet may push the user beyond the normal dose that he or she normally finds pleasurable, to the point where the user experiences unpleasant and dangerous side effects such as vomiting, depression, anxiety, severe dehydration, increased body temperature, and even death. So, if a regular user typically takes two or three Ecstasy tablets at the beginning of a rave party (anticipating that the concentration of MDMA in each tablet is low), and by random misfortune obtains Ecstasy tablets that contain high concentrations of MDMA, he or she may suffer severe medical consequences or even death as a result of an overdose.

SLANG TERMS FOR ECSTASY

Many drugs, both legal and illegal, have dozens of nicknames or "street" names, and Ecstasy is no exception. The list of nicknames for Ecstasy is long and constantly changing, and it can be difficult to find a comprehensive list anywhere in books or on the Internet. Some of the more common nicknames for Ecstasy and patterns of use, and the meanings behind these terms, are listed below.

Nickname	Meaning or origin
E	the first letter of Ecstasy
X	shorthand for the first syllable of Ecstasy
XTC	shorthand for the whole word Ecstasy
ADAM	an incorrect jumble of the abbreviation MDMA
love drug, hug drug, clarity, herbal bliss, E-bombs, lover's speed	Ecstasy-induced feelings of love and energy
pills, wafers, skittles, biscuits, sweettarts, beans, beanies, candy, rollies, vitamins	shape of the Ecstasy pill
gellies	Ecstasy in the form of a gel capsule
single, double, or triple stack	thickness of the Ecstasy pill or taking one, two, or three pills at a time
disco biscuit	reference to frequent use of Ecstasy at dance parties
hearts, butterflies, four-leaf clovers, letter biscuits	symbols that are imprinted on Ecstasy tablets
peep, peeper	Ecstasy user
rolling	being under the influence of Ecstasy
candy-flipping, trolling	combined use of Ecstasy and LSD

One kilogram of MDMA is enough to produce up to 10,000 Ecstasy tablets, depending on the concentration of MDMA used in each tablet.[3] Approximately half of each tablet is made up of MDMA, and the rest is made up

Nickname	Meaning or origin
elephant-flipping	combined use of Ecstasy and PCP
hippie-flipping	combined use of Ecstasy and psychedelic mushrooms
kitty-flipping	combined use of Ecstasy and ketamine
love-flipping	combined use of Ecstasy and mescaline
Nexus-flipping	combined use of Ecstasy and 2C-B
NoX	combined use of Ecstasy and nitrous oxide
Robo-flipping	combined use of Ecstasy and dextromethorphan (DXM, a common ingredient in over-the-counter cough syrups such as Robitussin that produces hallucinatory effects at high doses)
time-flipping	combined use of Ecstasy and DMT
sexstacy	combined use of Ecstasy and Viagra, since Ecstasy use can often result in impotence in males
Adam and Eve in the Garden of Eden	combined use of Ecstasy and MDEA
crazy-flipping	combined use of Ecstasy, LSD, cocaine, alprazolam (Xanax), alcohol, and marijuana
E-tards	An Ecstasy user who annoys other people by too much hugging or other touching behavior
E-puddle	An Ecstasy user laying on the floor exhausted from physical exertion
plugging	taking Ecstasy rectally

of inexpensive "filler" material such as cornstarch or cellulose, as is common practice in the production of many legal pharmaceuticals. However, Ecstasy tablets are often contaminated with other psychoactive substances such as amphetamine; methamphetamine; N-methyl-a-(1,3-benzodioxyl-5-yl)-2-butamine (MBDB); 4-methylthioamphetamine (4-MTA); meta-chlorophenylpiperazine (mCPP); or 2C-B; by-products of MDMA synthesis such as 3,4-methylenedioxyethylamphetamine (MDEA, often referred to as "Eve"), 3,4-methylenedioxyamphetamine (MDA), and paramethoxyamphetamine (PMA); caffeine; aspirin; ketamine; dextromethorphan (an ingredient in many cough suppressants); and even procaine or lidocaine (local anesthetics).[3] Such contaminants often cause Ecstasy users to become sick or experience unpleasant effects upon ingesting the tablets. Some Ecstasy pills contain no MDMA whatsoever, but other chemicals such as methamphetamine, MDEA, MDA, or PMA.[4] Several reports have shown that Ecstasy users who were under the impression they were taking Ecstasy tablets (containing MDMA) in fact ingested tablets that contained only PMA, MDBD, or 4-MTA, and this resulted in death.[5] Today, many rave parties are often attended by members of organizations such as DanceSafe and RaveSafe. The members of such organizations set up small booths at raves where Ecstasy users can have their tablets examined for MDMA content and impurities by simple chemical tests.

ECSTASY "BRAND" NAMES

Liquor stores and supermarkets sell numerous "brands" of legal drugs such as alcoholic beverages and cigarettes. During the turbulent 1960s when LSD use was at its highest, similar "brands" of the drug evolved, and often referred to popular culture icons and movies of the time such as Mickey Mouse, Snoopy, *Fantasia*, or *Alice in Wonderland*. During peak times of Ecstasy use in the past 20 years, brand names of Ecstasy also evolved, and many of these brands refer to the popular culture and corporate icons that are imprinted on the pills (i.e., Bart Simpsons, Volkswagens, etc.). These appealing logos are attempts by the manufacturers to establish favorites among users (similar to "brand loyalty" to specific brands of foods and products purchased from supermarkets), instill confidence in the product, and assert the notion that taking the drug is fun and harmless. Young users are further enticed by the candy-like bright coloring of the Ecstasy pills.[6]

Similar to magazines and Web sites that rate products such as cars and cell phones according to their popularity and performance, there are also

Web sites devoted to rating Ecstasy brands according to users' experience with the brand. Ecstasy sellers also are in the know about brands of Ecstasy. In a 2009 survey of 80 Ecstasy sellers, Micheline Duterte and colleagues found that the most popular brands of Ecstasy tablets were Mitsubishis, Alligators, Motorolas, Christmas Trees, No Names, and Blue Dolphins. Some of these Ecstasy sellers, however, did not regularly keep track of the specific brand or imprinted pills that they sold, because different brands were frequently mixed together in bags containing dozens or hundreds of pills. Rather, the sellers were more concerned with obtaining Ecstasy pills that were of high quality or purity, which can reduce undesirable side effects caused by contaminants.[7]

CHARACTERISTICS OF ECSTASY USERS

According to the recent National Survey on Drug Use and Health (NSDUH) survey that examined the usage of specific hallucinogens in the United States in 2006, Ecstasy is most frequently used by teenagers or young adults between the ages of 18 and 25. People between the ages of 12 and 17 are the second most frequent users of Ecstasy, followed by persons age 26 to 34, and finally 35 or older. In the 12- to 17-year age group, ecstasy was slightly more popular with females than males, but males age 18 to 25 used Ecstasy more frequently than females. This survey also revealed that of the three most frequently used hallucinogens (LSD, PCP, and Ecstasy), Ecstasy was most frequently tried for the first time in people over age 12, with more than 2 million new users in the year 2006 alone (see Figure 1.3). The number of people over the age of 12 who have tried Ecstasy at least once in their lifetime was approximately 12.6 million, or 4.6 percent of the population. However, among these three hallucinogens, approximately twice as many people age 12 or over have used LSD at least once in their lifetime as compared to Ecstasy.[8]

According to the 2003 National Household Survey on Drug Abuse (NHSDA), Ecstasy use is popular in many areas of the United States, especially in northeastern states such as New York and Massachussetts, western states such as California, Hawaii, and Arizona, and southern states such as Texas, the Carolinas, and Florida. Ecstasy use is least prevalent in midwestern states such as Indiana and Nebraska.[9] However, Ecstasy use patterns change by state on a yearly basis, and use patterns by state and other demographic variables

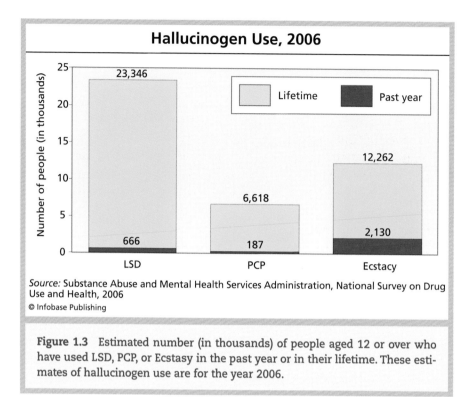

Hallucinogen Use, 2006

Source: Substance Abuse and Mental Health Services Administration, National Survey on Drug Use and Health, 2006

© Infobase Publishing

Figure 1.3 Estimated number (in thousands) of people aged 12 or over who have used LSD, PCP, or Ecstasy in the past year or in their lifetime. These estimates of hallucinogen use are for the year 2006.

are constantly monitored by the Drug Enforcement Administration and other government agencies.

Ecstasy is also popular in numerous countries around the world. According the 2003 NHSDA report, most Ecstasy users are of Caucasian or Asian descent, followed by people of Hispanic, African American and Native American descents. Ecstasy use is very rare among Islamic countries due to extremely strict Islam-based laws against drug and alcohol use. With regards to specific countries, the following percentages of national populations have tried Ecstasy between 1998 and 2002: Australia, 6.1%; Ireland, 2.4%; United Kingdom (England and Scotland), 2.2%; Spain, 1.8%; Belgium, 1.7%; Canada, 1.5; the Netherlands, 1.2%; Germany, 0.6%; and less than 0.5 percent in other countries including Mexico, Thailand, Poland, Denmark, the Czech Republic, Colombia, Israel, France, Italy, Bulgaria, and Russia. Of course, these data were obtained from national surveys from a decade ago, and it is likely that

HERBAL ECSTASY

In the early 2000s, a new drug called **herbal Ecstasy** surfaced and was promoted as a "natural" and "safer" alternative to MDMA as a way to experience energy, euphoria, and a potential way to help people lose weight. Until recently, herbal Ecstasy supplements were sold in health food and drug stores and marketed toward teenagers and young adults as being able to produce euphoria, increased energy, and heightened sexual sensations. They were also marketed as an aid in combating asthma. Common names for herbal Ecstasy were Cloud 9, Rave Energy, X, Herbal X, Ultimate X-phoria, and Herbal Bliss.

Herbal Ecstasy is actually nothing more than a stimulant containing **ephedrine** (a stimulant similar to pseudoephedrine found in many over-the-counter nasal decongestants) and caffeine. The manufacturers of herbal Ecstasy claimed the product was "natural" because the ephedrine it contained was derived from the Chinese herb Ephedra (also called "ma huang") or other ephedrine extracts, and the caffeine it contained came from the kola nut. Herbal Ecstasy also contained other herbs like ginseng, ginko biloba, green tea, and nutmeg. However, in the early 2000s, an increasing number of medical reports indicated that people taking herbal Ecstasy were suffering from irregular heartbeats, heart attacks, strokes, and seizures. These events were more likely to occur in people with heart conditions, those who were taking antidepressants, or those who were overly sensitive to stimulants. In 2004, the U.S. Food and Drug Administration (FDA) banned the sale of ephedrine-containing dietary supplements and Ephedra. However, this ban did not prohibit the sale of prescription drugs that contained synthetic ephedrine or traditional Chinese herbal remedies and teas.

some of these figures have changed since then. For example, a recent survey of Ecstasy users in Australia showed that the percent of the population that has used Ecstasy at least once in their lifetime has steadily risen from 2.5 percent in 1995 to almost 9 percent in 2007.

THE RAVE CULTURE

The use of Ecstasy in the United States peaked between 1998 and 2002, as did the popularity of rave parties. As a result, the use of Ecstasy has become almost synonymous with all-night rave parties, which are usually held in empty warehouses or other large buildings. At a typical rave party, many teenagers and young adults gather and dance to high-energy "techno" and electronic dance music. Here they buy and drink alcohol, smoke marijuana, or take hallucinogens such as Ecstasy, sometimes in numerous combinations. Rave parties are usually densely packed with hundreds, and sometimes thousands, of people. One rave held in the Netherlands was attended by approximately 14,000 people.[10] Raves usually begin at night and last until the following morning, although some last 48 hours or longer. The stimulant properties of Ecstasy and other drugs such as methamphetamine allow the youngsters to

Figure 1.4 The use of Ecstasy has become synonymous with all-night raves. (*Shutterstock*)

dance for hours on end. Accompanying the loud dance music are flashing and moving colored lights, people carrying "glow-sticks" or other fluorescent neon-colored items. Oftentimes the environment becomes overly hot, and since Ecstasy is known to produce hyperthermia and dehydration on its own, there are "cooling" rooms with water fans, and ice where people can go to cool off and rehydrate themselves. The entactogenic and euphoria-producing properties of Ecstasy make the rave environment a happy place where complete strangers dance, socialize, and even hug each other.

SUMMARY

Ecstasy/MDMA is an illegal hallucinogen and stimulant that is chemically related to methamphetamine. It is primarily taken by teenagers and young adults at rave parties or other social gatherings. It intensifies physical sensations and perceptions and produces heightened self-esteem and sociability along with profound feelings of euphoria, love, and empathy. The remainder of this book will discuss in detail the history of Ecstasy use, the biological and psychological effects of Ecstasy as well as the medical consequences of long-term use, the addictive potential of Ecstasy, and ways to treat Ecstasy dependence or overdose. Finally, current social and legal issues surrounding Ecstasy, such as its legalization for use as an aid in psychotherapy and Ecstasy chemical testing stations at raves, will be examined.

2
History of Ecstasy

Often called the "father" or "grandfather" of Ecstasy, biochemist Dr. Alexander Shulgin is one of the most famous "self-testers" of hallucinogens. He first described the psychological effects of Ecstasy in a 1978 article in which he noted that the drug could produce "an easily controlled altered state of consciousness with emotional and sensual overtones."[1] He further stated in this article that "there are few physical indicators of intoxication, and psychological sequelae are virtually non-existent" (more recent evidence to the contrary will be presented in Chapters 3 and 4). Shulgin did not find his initial experience with Ecstasy to be as "transformative" as he did with other more powerful hallucinogens such as LSD, since Ecstasy did not produce extremely vivid visual or auditory hallucinations. In fact, he compared the effects of Ecstasy to that of a "low-calorie martini." Shulgin was, however, intrigued by the ability of Ecstasy to produce a loss of normal social inhibitions and a sense of "clarity", and the fact that it "opened up a person, both to other people and inner thoughts, but didn't necessarily color it with pretty colors and strange noises." Because of this, Shulgin conceived the notion that Ecstasy could potentially be used in psychotherapy, and suggested this to some of his colleagues who were either psychiatrists or psychologists. One of these psychiatrists, Dr. George Greer, found that Ecstasy produced enormous beneficial effects in his patients due to its ability to lower patients' defenses and therefore allow them to face troubling, even repressed, memories. Greer tested Ecstasy on dozens of patients, and stated that "without exception, every therapist who I talked to or even heard of, every therapist who gave MDMA to a patient, was highly impressed by the results."[2]

THE DISCOVERY OF ECSTASY

Over the years, scientific journals and books have reported some incorrect facts regarding the initial discovery of MDMA. Some report it as being first synthesized in 1912, others in 1914. Some state it was intended for use in soldiers in World War I, and other state it was intended to be a weight loss drug. Recently, several scientists at the Germany-based pharmaceutical company Merck, whose scientists are credited with discovering MDMA, performed extensive research of the company's historical research archives in order to clarify the confusion.[3]

At the time when the molecule that would later be called MDMA was first identified, Drs. Walter Beckh, Otto Wolfes, and Anton Köllisch were attempting to synthesize new drugs that could be used to promote blot clotting and wound healing (called **styptic** drugs), and which could be of use in treating bleeding disorders such as **hemophilia** or to control bleeding after being wounded in combat. Existing styptic drugs included hydrastine and hydrastinine, but these were derived from rare plants that were difficult and expensive to obtain. In addition, another German pharmaceutical company called Bayer/Farbenfabriken Elberfeld already held patents on certain ways to synthesize these styptic drugs, which forced scientists at Merck to look for new ways to synthetically make hydrastine and hydrastinine or related drugs.

With some hard work, Drs. Beckh, Wolfes, and colleagues came up-with a new method to synthesize a molecule closely related to hydrastinine called 3-methyl-hydrastinine, which they hoped would be as effective a styptic agent as regular hydrastinine (and, it turns out, it was). In this newly developed method for synthesizing 3-methyl-hydrastinine, one of the molecules generated in the process was MDMA, although at the time it was referred to in the laboratory records as "Methylsafrylamin." Due to its positive styptic effects, Merck filed a patent application (Patent No. 274350) with the German Imperial Patent office in Berlin on

GOVERNMENT AND MILITARY TESTING OF PSYCHEDELIC DRUGS

Law enforcement and government intelligence agencies have long been interested in mind-altering substances and the potential to use them during interrogation of crime suspects, captured enemy soldiers, or foreign spies. In various projects spanning several decades, agencies such as the Central Intelligence Agency (CIA) have conducted studies on people in an attempt to find a **truth drug** or **truth serum**—a psychoactive substance that would cause a person being interrogated to reveal secret information that he or she would normally withhold for fear of being detained, jailed, or harmed.

One of the first of these programs was termed Project CHATTER, which was initiated by the U.S. Navy in 1947. Project CHATTER involved the use of the hallucinogenic drug mescaline, which had been used on inmates at a Nazi concentration camp during World War II for the same purposes. However, the Navy found mescaline to be an ineffective truth serum and terminated the project six years later. In Project BLUEBIRD, the CIA gave people sedatives such as barbiturates with the hypothesis being that a person in a heavily sedated and confused state of mind might unwillingly reveal information. However, this research yielded no particularly promising results, as the experimental subjects babbled nothing but gibberish when asked questions

December 24, 1912, to use 3-methyl-hydrastinine to control bleeding as well as the methods for its chemical synthesis. It should be noted that *nowhere* in this patent application, or other related patents filed by Merck, was it mentioned that Methylsafrylamin or 3-methyl-hydrastinine were to be used as appetite suppressants or weight loss drugs. The patent was approved on May 16, 1914.[4]

In 1927 (the year the original patent was set to expire), Merck scientist Dr. Max Oberlin noted that the molecular structure of Methylsafrylamin was somewhat similar to that of adrenaline and ephetonine (also known as ephedrine, a stimulant), and Merck had an interest in developing drugs about specific information. Project BLUEBIRD changed its name to Project ARTICHOKE in 1951. At this time, the CIA conducted mock interrogations by telling military officers not to reveal a particular piece of information, then administering LSD and interrogating them to see if they would divulge the information. An initial series of these mock interrogations showed that officers under the influence of LSD would indeed reveal secret information, yet have no knowledge of doing so after the effects of LSD had worn off. But further studies showed that LSD did not always produce the desired effect. Sometimes the person being interrogated would be inaccurate due to the fact that LSD was causing the person to experience significant anxiety and panic, or to completely lose touch with reality.

In 1953, CIA director Allen Dulles initiated Project MK-ULTRA, one of the CIA's biggest programs on drug-induced mind control. In these experiments, instead of administering LSD or other mind-altering substances knowingly to a subject in a laboratory setting, the drug was given to unwitting subjects in natural settings such as in their home or at a bar. As expected, the victims would begin to experience hallucinations, but often these hallucinations would turn frightening because the victim was unaware of having ingested any hallucinogenic substance. This research generally found that the effects of LSD were too unreliable and unpredictable to yield information from drugged subjects.

related to these molecules. Oberlin tested Methylsafrylamin (in his notes he referred to it as "Safrylmethylamin") for its ability to constrict blood vessels and the uterus. Safrylmethylamin was very effective in these tests, but also showed a high amount of **toxicity** (dying of tissue or cells). Despite his results, Merck officials ordered Oberlin to cease his work on Safrylmethylamin until further notice, citing the increasing prices in making the drug as the primary reason.

Following Oberlin's work, there is no mention of Methylsafrylamin or Safrylmethylamin in Merck's historical archives until 1952 when Merck chemist Dr. Albert van Schoor conducted a simple experiment on flies to further explore its toxic effects. He noted that after 30 minutes of exposure of Methylsafrylamin vapors, flies began to lay on their backs and eventually died. There was no evidence that van Schoor tested Methylsafrylamin on humans.

In 1953 and 1954, the U.S. Army, in collaboration with the University of Michigan, conducted confidential tests of MDMA (under the code name EA-1475) and other psychologically active drugs such as mescaline in several animal species including dogs, cats, rats, mice, guinea pigs, and monkeys. The goal of these experiments was to determine what the lethal dose of each drug was as well as its effects motor ability, heart rate, etc. The results of these military-sponsored experiments showed that MDMA was not toxic to the brain, although many later studies have shown that MDMA can cause significant damage to nerve cells in the brain. In addition, MDMA was found to be less toxic to other organs than its chemical cousin MDA. Although these experiments were conducted in the 1950s, the results were not made public until 1973.[5]

In 1959, Merck chemist Dr. Wolfgang Fruhstorfer was interested in developing new stimulants in cooperation with other scientists involved in "aviation medicine" (i.e., giving medications such as stimulants to pilots to increase their alertness and keep them from getting fatigued on long missions). Fruhstorfer worked with Methylsafrylamin and several related molecules, but Merck's archives never indicated whether he tested these substances in humans.

ENTER DR. ALEXANDER SHULGIN

In 1960, a group of Polish scientists described a new way to synthesize MDMA in a scientific journal, which represented the first time that the means for making MDMA were publicly accessible.[6] Only a few years later, Dr. Alexander Shulgin (nicknamed "Sasha"), a chemist at Dow Chemical Company, also synthesized MDMA. Although Shulgin is often credited with the discovery of the potential therapeutic uses of MDMA, a psychotherapist named Dr. Leo Zeff was actually the first to combine MDMA with psychotherapy in 1976.[7] Zeff conducted numerous therapy sessions after giving his patients MDMA, and frequently referred to it as "Adam," a close but incorrect anagram of the chemical abbreviation for Ecstasy.[8] Zeff feared the Drug Enforcement Administration (DEA) might not react kindly to his regular use of MDMA in psychotherapy and therefore decided to keep his use of the drug in therapy quiet and unpublished.[9] However, soon the news of the potential promising effects of MDMA in psychotherapy spread to other psychiatrists and psychologists, and two years after Zeff first utilized the drug, Shulgin published a report on the psychological effects of MDMA in 1978.[10] Shulgin then conveyed his positive experiences with MDMA to some colleagues who were psychotherapists, and proposed to them that the ability of MDMA to produce feelings of love, empathy, and openness to others might be of potential use in "breaking down" psychological barriers between the patient and therapist. In addition to its empathogenic and entactogenic effects, MDMA also inhibits feelings of fear, and psychotherapists argued that people undergoing psychological therapy might feel less emotional vulnerability and therefore form stronger bonds and feelings of trust with their therapists and make greater progress in solving their psychological problems.[11]

Shulgin eventually left his job at Dow Chemical Company to pursue his own interests. He engaged in several activities, including work as a private consultant and lecturer at various universities in the San Francisco Bay Area. Through an acquaintance and DEA employee named Bob Sager, Shulgin established a rapport with the DEA and taught classes on psychoactive drugs to DEA agents. The DEA permitted Shulgin to establish a laboratory and analyze various chemical samples obtained from drug seizures, including Schedule I controlled substances. Shulgin was allowed a great deal of freedom in his laboratory, and he and his wife Ann eventually began synthesizing and testing the effects of hundreds of psychoactive drugs on themselves and others. He even developed a way of ranking the psychedelic effects of the various drugs, known as the Shulgin Rating Scale. Many of these drugs Shulgin tested on themselves and others fell in the chemical category of phenethylamines. In 1991, Shulgin published a book entitled *Phenethylamines I Have Known and Loved* (or PIHKAL, for short), in which he documented in great detail his experiences with self-experimenting psychedelic substances, including MDMA, as well as the chemical means to synthesize such drugs.[12] Two years later, the DEA raided his lab, found discrepancies in his laboratory record keeping, forced Shulgin to give up his Schedule I controlled substance license, and

Figure 2.1 Dr. Alexander Shulgin, a chemist well known for experimenting with psychedelic drugs including MDMA. (*Corbis*)

fined him $25,000 for possession of chemical samples that were not sent to him by the DEA.

THE SPREAD OF ECSTASY PRODUCTION AND DISTRIBUTION

In 1972, a decade after the publication of methods for synthesis of MDMA, the first reports of seizures of Ecstasy tablets on the streets of Chicago were reported.[13] Following Shulgin's proclamation of the wonders of MDMA use in the late 1970s, groups of chemists began to form and synthesize MDMA in pill form. One of the first of these groups to form was in Boston. Known as the "Boston Group,"[14] this group first commercialized MDMA under the name "Ecstasy" in 1981, and soon its distribution spread to other states. In 1983, an offshoot of the Boston Group formed in Texas (the "Texas Group") and launched a mass synthesis of MDMA pills and tablets.[15] The pills could

HISTORY OF MDMA'S COUSIN, MDA

The chemical structure of methylenedioxyamphetamine (MDA) is very similar to that of MDMA. It was first synthesized by German chemists in 1910 but not tested in living animals until 1939.[16] In the first tests, MDA was shown to produce stimulant properties including increased heart rate, breathing, and stimulation of the central nervous system.[17] Two years later, MDA was administered to patients with **Parkinson's disease** (a debilitating disease of the nervous system with symptoms such as trembling of the arms, hands, or legs and involuntary movements) but it was reported that the drug made the symptoms of this disease worse.[18] The U.S. military subsequently developed an interest in the drug as a possible truth serum and recruited several psychiatrists at the New York State Psychiatric Institute to administer it to patients. These drugs were classified as belonging to the Edgewood Arsenal, and given code names "EA" followed by several numbers. MDA was one of these drugs, and was given the code name EA-1298. In 1953, MDA was given on several occasions to a patient. An intravenous dose of 500 mg of MDA was lethal to the patient, and the U.S. military subsequently abandoned further research on the drug.[19] However, other researchers and pharmaceutical companies retained their interest in the drug, patenting it as a cough or appetite suppressant or a sedative. In 1959, G. A. Alles intentionally ingested MDA and described its ability to increase self-awareness and the intensity of certain sensations.[20] MDA was also reported to increase feelings of empathy, and some researchers recommended that it, like MDMA, might be useful in psychological therapy.[21] However, throughout the 1960s, MDA use and abuse became widespread, and in 1970 the Drug Enforcement Administration classified the drug as a Schedule I substance, indicating that it had no medical value and high potential for addiction (see Appendix) and therefore illegal to synthesize, possess, transport, sell, or use.

be bought openly at bars and dance clubs and could even be purchased with credit cards. The ensuing increase in recreational use of MDMA caused a great deal of concern among the therapists who backed its use in psychotherapy for fear that the drug might be misused. In addition, the DEA became concerned over increasing numbers of Ecstasy tablet seizures. As a result, on July 27, 1984, the DEA recommended that MDMA be classified as a Schedule I controlled substance.[22]

By definition, this classification of MDMA as a Schedule I controlled substance would have made it illegal to synthesize, possess, transport, sell, or use the drug, and assign it a status of having no medical value. Of course, psychotherapists who used MDMA in their practice vehemently opposed the DEA's recommendation, which ultimately led to various scheduled legal hearings in 1985 on its therapeutic value versus potential for harm. On May 31, 1985, just 10 days prior to the commencement of the first of these hearings, the DEA classified MDMA as a Schedule I controlled substance for a one-year period effective July 1 of the same year, as it was deemed an "imminent hazard to public safety."[23]

Ironically, in 1985, MDMA gained tremendous popularity on the Spanish island of Ibiza, where it was combined with all-night parties of dance music, flashing and moving lights, and alcohol and other drugs. College-aged tourists who visited Ibiza nicknamed it "XTC Island" and found these all-night dance parties to be highly enjoyable. Tourists would subsequently return home to countries in Europe and North America and hold dance parties (along with the distribution of MDMA), and the "rave" culture was born.

ECSTASY IS MADE ILLEGAL

The testimonials of numerous psychiatrists and psychotherapists who claimed that MDMA had great potential value for use in psychological therapy, and their insistence that making the drug illegal would hinder further research, persuaded the judicial committee in charge of the 1985 hearings to recommend that MDMA be classified as a Schedule III controlled substance, with an accepted medical value and low potential for abuse or addiction. However, the head administrator of the DEA rejected this recommendation and classified MDMA as a Schedule I controlled substance on November 13, 1986. An appeal by a physician by the name of Dr. Lester Grinspoon temporarily reversed this classification on December 22, 1987, but the DEA quickly reverted the classification back to Schedule I on March 23, 1988, and it has remained

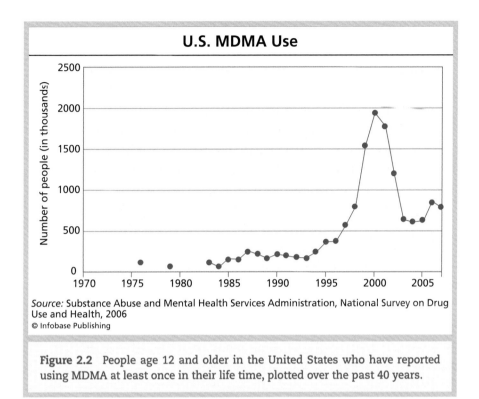

Figure 2.2 People age 12 and older in the United States who have reported using MDMA at least once in their life time, plotted over the past 40 years.

in this category ever since.[24] However, there has been a recent renewal in the debate over the medical value of MDMA.

CONTINUED USE DESPITE ILLEGALIZATION

Although MDMA was outlawed by the DEA in the late 1980s, a 1987 survey of college students on university campuses such as Stanford University indicated that as many as 39 percent of students had tried MDMA at least once.[25] Throughout the 1990s, the use of MDMA continued to rise dramatically in the United States and other countries, peaking with a 71 percent surge in use in the years 1998–2002 (see Figure 2.2). A parallel peak in the number of Ecstasy tablets seized also occurred during these years, with the U.S. Customs Service reporting 750,000 tablets seized in 1998 and 9.3 million in 2000.[26] However, after 2002, a substantial drop in MDMA use has been observed, and the number of people using MDMA has remained relatively stable in the past half decade. The reasons for this decline in MDMA use can possibly be attributed to the success of antidrug campaigns, such as a campaign specifically designed to educate teenagers and college students about the dangers of Ecstasy use that was initiated by the Partnership for a Drug-Free America in 2002. In addition to this educational campaign, which may have changed the perception of Ecstasy as a "fun" and "safe" drug to one with possible dangerous effects, numerous reports of ecstasy-related health emergencies and deaths caught the attention of the mainstream media during the early 2000s, which likely has deterred people from using Ecstasy.

SUMMARY

MDMA was first chemically synthesized by German scientists in 1912 at the pharmaceutical company Merck in a series of studies on developing drugs to aid in blood clotting. Despite common assertations to the contrary, MDMA was not developed as an appetite suppressant or weight loss drug. It was not until the 1950s when MDMA was actually tested by scientists and the U.S. military on animals and humans for its toxic and physiological effects. The psychedelic, empathogenic, and entactogenic effects of MDMA were first reported in the 1970s. Numerous scientists, psychiatrists, and psychological counselors felt that MDMA could be of great benefit to patients undergoing psychotherapy so as to break down people's fears and emotional barriers. However, MDMA began to be used recreationally and during the early 1980s a mass underground production of MDMA tablets began to surface. Because of growing fears of potential harmful effects of the drug, the DEA made MDMA illegal in 1986. Despite the criminalization of the drug, recreational MDMA use increased dramatically during the 1990s and peaked in the years 1998–2002, where it became very popular at rave dances. Since then, MDMA use has declined and subsequently remained relatively stable, perhaps due to successful educational campaigns by antidrug organizations and the publicity of deaths resulting from its use.

3

Psychological and Biological Effects of Ecstasy

Jeff was a 19-year-old college student when his friends invited him to a rave party. Not long after arriving at the party he ingested a double stack (two pills) of Ecstasy, as suggested by his friends since he wanted to get a "really good experience" during his first time using the drug. After 12 hours of dancing and socializing, Jeff felt the effects of Ecstasy starting to wear off, so he bought and swallowed another double stack. He did this again another 12 hours later. After approximately 30 hours at the rave party, Jeff suddenly collapsed onto the floor. His friends called an ambulance, which transported him to the emergency department at a local hospital. The paramedics reported that Jeff was incoherent and could not answer any of their questions. Upon arrival at the emergency room (ER), a nurse took his vital signs. He had an elevated body temperature of 102.2°F (normal is approximately 98.6°F), blood pressure 140/96 mm Hg (normal is approximately 115/75), his resting heart rate was 128 beats per minute (normal is 60–100), and his respiratory rate was 24 breaths per minute (normal is approximately 12). Jeff's facial skin appeared flushed (red) and sweaty, his pupils were dilated, and he was extremely dehydrated. The ER nurse took a blood sample from Jeff's arm and sent it to the hospital's blood laboratory for analysis. Initial results showed that Jeff had intoxicating levels of alcohol in his blood and traces of amphetamines, which were later confirmed to be MDMA. The ER staff then proceeded to give Jeff intravenous saline to help him become rehydrated, and gave him a dose of dantrolene (a muscle relaxant) to help bring down his high body temperature. Jeff was kept in the hospital for three days to monitor his hydration status and body temperature. He was later released from the hospital and referred to the substance abuse services center of his college's health center.

The preceding story about Jeff is based on a true case report published in the *Journal of the American Board of Family Practice.*[1] Ecstasy (MDMA) is a hallucinogen and stimulant that has numerous effects on the brain and various other systems in the body. Before discussing how MDMA acts within the body, particularly the brain, to produce its stimulant, hallucinogenic, empathogenic, and entactogenic effects, a brief overview of how nerve cells work is needed.

HOW NERVE CELLS IN THE BRAIN WORK

In the brain, **neurons** or nerve cells carry electrical signals along wire-like nerve fibers called **axons**. Axons can range from less than a millimeter in length to up to several centimeters. At the end of each axon is a mushroom-shaped nerve ending called a **synaptic terminal**. When the electrical signal traveling down the axon reaches the synaptic terminal, it causes chemical messengers, called **neurotransmitters** (such as **serotonin**), which are normally stored in sphere-like packages called **vesicles**, to be released and secreted onto nearby neurons. This junction between a synaptic terminal and a nearby neuron is called a **synapse**. There are billions of synapses in the brain, and each neuron can have as many as 10,000 different synapses on it. After neurotransmitters are released, they diffuse away from the synaptic terminal into the synapse and encounter proteins called **receptors** on the surface of nearby neurons. Receptors are specific proteins that are designed to recognize specific neurotransmitters. Receptors are usually located on **dendrites**, which are branched fibers designed to receive numerous signals from other neurons, or on the **cell body** of the neuron, which contains various cell components including genetic material (i.e., chromosomes composed of DNA) that is found in the **nucleus** (see Figure 3.1.). When activated by neurotransmitters, these receptors can cause the nerve cell on which they reside to either become activated (so it passes along the electrical signal) or inhibited (so it does not pass the signal along). The chemical signal between the neurons is terminated by proteins called **transporters**, which reabsorb

Neuron

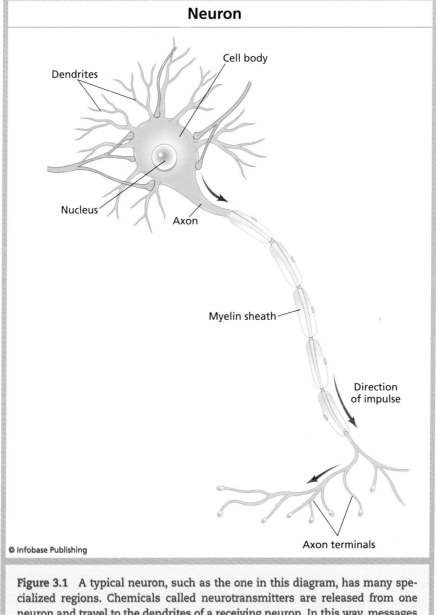

Dendrites

Cell body

Nucleus

Axon

Myelin sheath

Direction of impulse

Axon terminals

© Infobase Publishing

Figure 3.1 A typical neuron, such as the one in this diagram, has many specialized regions. Chemicals called neurotransmitters are released from one neuron and travel to the dendrites of a receiving neuron. In this way, messages are passed from neuron to neuron in the brain.

the neurotransmitter back into the synaptic terminal, where it no longer can interact with the receptors on the nearby neuron, and can be repackaged into vesicles for use again in later nerve signals.

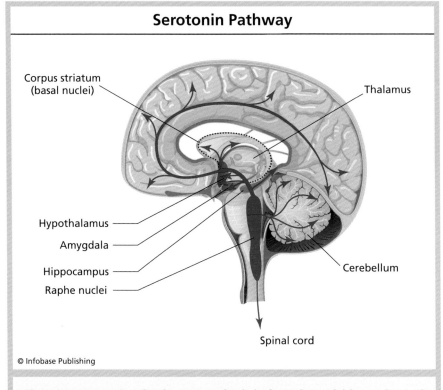

Serotonin Pathway

Corpus striatum
(basal nuclei)

Thalamus

Hypothalamus

Amygdala

Hippocampus

Raphe nuclei

Cerebellum

Spinal cord

© Infobase Publishing

Figure 3.2 Serotonin-releasing neurons begin in the raphe nuclei, but project and release serotonin throughout most of the brain. Targets of these neurons include the hippocampus, which is involved in memory, and the amygdala, which is involved in emotions. This diagram shows the pathways of serotonin in the brain.

ECSTASY CHANGES BRAIN CHEMISTRY

MDMA affects the chemical signaling between neurons in the brain in two different ways. First, MDMA causes neurons that use serotonin as their neurotransmitter to produce a massive release of this chemical, regardless of whether or not electrical signals are being carried by the axon. The result is a flooding of the brain's synapses with serotonin. In addition to producing this massive release of serotonin, MDMA also inhibits the activity of the transporters that normally reabsorb the serotonin back into the synaptic terminal. This has a "double whammy" effect on the chemistry of the brain—MDMA causes the flooding of synapses in numerous regions of the brain with serotonin, and this effect is long lasting because MDMA also inhibits transporters from reabsorbing the serotonin back into the synaptic terminal. MDMA has similar effects on synaptic terminals that use the neurotransmitters dopamine and norepinephrine, which likely contribute to its stimulant-like effects. MDMA can also increase the release of the neurotransmitter acetylcholine, and can bind directly to specific types of receptors for serotonin, acetylcholine, and norepinephrine. However, MDMA exerts its most potent effects on serotonin-containing synaptic terminals.[2]

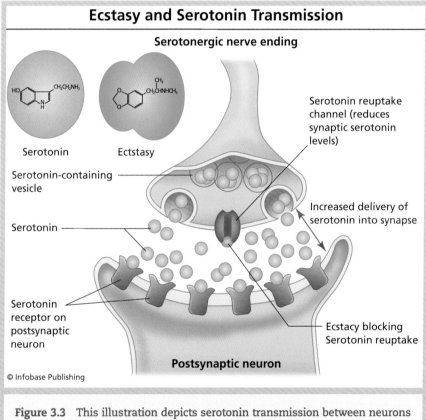

Ecstasy and Serotonin Transmission

Serotonergic nerve ending

Serotonin

Ectstasy

Serotonin reuptake channel (reduces synaptic serotonin levels)

Serotonin-containing vesicle

Increased delivery of serotonin into synapse

Serotonin

Serotonin receptor on postsynaptic neuron

Ecstacy blocking Serotonin reuptake

Postsynaptic neuron

© Infobase Publishing

Figure 3.3 This illustration depicts serotonin transmission between neurons and Ecstasy's effects on that transmission. Ecstasy causes a massive outpouring of serotonin into the synapse and also blocks the reabsorption of serotonin back into the axon terminal, resulting in a long-lasting flooding of synapses in the brain with serotonin.

THE BRAIN AND ITS SEROTONIN SYSTEMS

The brain has numerous regions that are each specialized for particular functions. So the effect a particular drug has on a person's thinking or behavior may depend in which brain region it is acting. Table 3.1 describes the different functions of some of the main regions of the human brain; Figure 3.3 presents a diagram of the brain. This figure also shows the widespread distribution of serotonin-containing synaptic terminals throughout the human brain. It is therefore not surprising that MDMA produces a variety of psychological and physiological effects.

METABOLISM OF MDMA

MDMA typically reaches its peak concentrations in the blood approximately two hours after ingestion, which coincides with the time in which the peak psychological effects are experienced. It takes the body approximately nine hours to metabolize the amount of MDMA ingested (known as the **half-life**). However, in the liver, one of the metabolites of MDMA that is generated is 3,4-methylenedioxyamphetamine (MDA). Because it has stimulant properties of its own, MDA is called an **active metabolite**. MDA levels in the blood peak about 13 hours after initial ingestion of MDMA, and MDA has a half-life of approximately 24 hours. So, while the initial effects of MDMA may peak within two hours after taking the drug and start to wear off after nine to 10 hours, the active metabolite MDA is present in the body for much longer periods of time. This may explain how Ecstasy users can dance and remain awake for very long periods of time (48 hours or more).[3]

MDMA and MDA are also metabolized to form chemicals such as 3,4-dihydroxymethamphetamine (HHMA), 4-hydroxy-3-methoxymethamphetamine (HMMA), 3,4-dyhydroxyamphetamine (HHA) and 4-hydroxy-3-mcthoxyamphetamine (HMA). All of these chemicals are eventually metabolized to molecules related to the amino acid glycine, and are excreted in the urine. One interesting feature of MDMA is its ability to inhibit the activity of one of the enzymes that is responsible for its metabolism. The MDMA molecule can form a complex with a liver enzyme called CYP2D6, which reduces the ability of this enzyme to further metabolize MDMA. This process is known as autoinhibition and is partly responsible for the relatively long half-life of MDMA.[4]

Table 3.1 Main Regions of the Brain and Their Function	
Region	Function
cerebrum	largest part of the brain, consisting of a left and right hemisphere
cerebral cortex	outermost wrinkled part of the brain where planning, thinking, and information processes occurs
corpus callosum	bundle of nerve fibers that connects the left and right hemispheres of the cerebrum
pineal gland	controls biological rhythms such as sleeping and waking, secretes the hormone melatonin
cerebellum	controls motor coordination and balance
medulla oblongata, pons, and midbrain	control basic bodily functions like chewing, swallowing, heart rate, motivation, and breathing; collectively known as the "brainstem"
pituitary gland	secretes hormones that control many bodily functions such as growth, metabolism, and reproduction
hypothalamus	controls metabolism, sleeping, hunger, thirst, and body temperature
thalamus	acts as a relay station for all incoming information from the senses (touch, vision, hearing, etc.)

PSYCHOLOGICAL EFFECTS

The psychological effects of Ecstasy are the primary reason people take the drug. In the dose range of 50 to 150 mg, Ecstasy produces numerous pleasurable effects, including feelings of love, peace, relaxation, affection, friendliness, humor, closeness to and intimacy to others, open-mindedness, a greater ability to empathize and understand other's feelings (**empathogenesis**), and a sense of unity with others and the world around them (**entactogenesis**). It also produces feelings of extreme happiness, exhilaration and well-being (**euphoria**), and Ecstasy users who have been interviewed about

DRUG HALF-LIVES

Drugs are often referred to as "short-acting" or "long-lasting" based on their half-life, which is the amount of time it takes for the body to metabolize and/or excrete a substance after it has been ingested. For example, the half-life of MDMA is approximately nine hours, which means if a person took Ecstasy and achieved a peak blood concentration of 10 milligrams of MDMA per deciliter (mg/dl) of blood, it would take nine hours for that concentration to be reduced to 5 mg/dl. However, it does not take just two half-lives for the body to rid itself of a substance entirely. After an additional nine hours, the concentration of MDMA would be 2.5 mg/dl, then in another nine hours it would be 1.25 mg/dl, and so on. Therefore, it can take many half-lives for the body to metabolize or excrete a drug to a point where it is no longer detectable in the blood. Different drugs have different half-lives— MDMA has a half-life of approximately nine hours, whereas that of methamphetamine is slightly longer at around 12 hours. Some drugs have a very long half-life, such as marijuana, whose psychoactive ingredients and metabolites have half-lives in excess of 24 hours, whereas shorter acting drugs such as nicotine and cocaine have half-lives of about one hour. Not only can the half-life of a particular drug influence how long its psychological and physiological effects last, but also how long it can be detected in the blood in the event that the drug user needs to undergo a drug test for employment, eligibility for participation in sports, etc.

their experiences with the drug report feelings like "All I wanted to do was smile" and "I don't think that anything could have brought be down. I loved it." In some individuals Ecstasy can produce feeling of increases spiritual awareness. Ecstasy also has the ability to reduce people's fears, sensitivity to criticisms, anxieties and concerns, feelings of alienation from others, as well as lower people's "defenses" so that they feel uninhibited toward being close to others, even total strangers. Ecstasy also can cause people to become more "chatty" or talkative. Since Ecstasy tends to "relax" the mind, people who have taken Ecstasy often lose the desire to concentrate or perform complex mental tasks and just "be." Ecstasy is a stimulant and produces feelings of increased energy and endurance.[5]

Another motivating factor for taking Ecstasy is to experience its ability to produce mild hallucinations. Ecstasy enhances the sensory perception of lights, touch, sounds, and music. Ecstasy users have described these experiences with phrases such as "being touched was so intense" and "I felt I had a stereo inside my body." The hallucinatory effects of Ecstasy are likely a result of direct stimulation of a specific type of serotonin receptor (called the 5-HT_2 receptor) by the MDMA molecule. This receptor is also known to be stimulated directly by more potent hallucinogens such as LSD and mescaline. However, the hallucinatory effects of MDMA are qualitatively different than those induced by LSD and mescaline, the latter of which can consist of extremely bizarre mental and visual imagery and out-of-body experiences (called **depersonalization**).[6]

However, not everyone who takes Ecstasy has an enjoyable psychological experience. Some people can experience unpleasant psychological effects such as feeling lonely, depressed or sad, anxious or jittery, paranoid, or irritable. Other negative psychological effects can include memory loss and amnesia, decreased libido or impotence (in males), and mood swings. There are several factors that may cause negative psychological experiences with Ecstasy. The first is the user's expectations—if he or she had a prior negative experience using the drug or perhaps with a specific "brand" of Ecstasy, the user is more likely to have another negative experience. Similarly, if a person is in a bad mood immediately prior to taking Ecstasy, he or she is more likely to have an unpleasant experience with the drug. A particularly important factor that can contribute to producing a negative psychological experience after taking Ecstasy is the dosage. People who take higher doses of MDMA, usually greater than 150 mg at a time, are more likely to have negative psychological experiences than those who take lower doses. People who take very high doses of the drug (i.e., 200 mg and above) may experience an overdose, sometimes called **acute MDMA toxicity**. This toxicity is characterized by adverse psychological symptoms such as aggression, confusion, delirium, panic attacks, **psychosis** (loss of touch with reality), and numerous physiological and medical complications. Other factors such as taking Ecstasy in combination with alcohol, the presence of contaminants in Ecstasy pills such as methamphetamine or MDA, and a genetic predisposition to metabolizing MDMA abnormally can contribute to negative experiences with the drug.[7]

There are also known gender differences in the psychological effects of Ecstasy. The psychological effects of MDMA tend to be more intense in females than in males. These differences include both the positive psychological effects (feelings of joy, being at one with their surroundings, and intensified physical sensations) as well as the negative psychological effects (inability to concentrate, fear of losing control over their bodies, and feelings of anxiety and depression). Females also tend to experience a more severe "crash" than males. However, the physiological and medical complications resulting from MDMA overdose, including death, are usually greater in males than females.[8]

When the psychological effects of MDMA start to wear off as a result of the body's metabolic breakdown of the drug, Ecstasy users frequently experience what is commonly referred to as the "crash", or "coming down." This phase of the Ecstasy experience is dominated by feelings of irritability, depression, anxiety, and even anger and hostility, and can last for several days. The crash may be a strong motivating factor for taking another dose of MDMA. The reason females undergo a more severe crash than males is possibly related to the fact that females tend to be more vocal about changes in bodily symptoms and more prone to depression and anxiety than males, or to differences in metabolism of MDMA.[9]

PHYSIOLOGICAL EFFECTS

MDMA does not just have potent effects on the brain—it acts in numerous other systems in the body, and many of these effects can be harmful or fatal. MDMA often causes feelings of nausea and vomiting (also known as **emesis**), especially when taken at higher doses. Like its chemical cousin methamphetamine, MDMA is a stimulant and results in long-lasting increases in heart rate (called **tachycardia**), blood pressure (called **hypertension**), shakiness, restlessness, dilation of the pupils (called **mydriasis**), and excessive sweating (also called **diaphoresis**). These effects are primarily a result of the ability of MDMA to increase the release of adrenaline, noradrenaline, and dopamine. MDMA also causes thickening (**coagulation**) of the blood. When coagulation becomes significant and is combined with prolonged tachycardia (i.e., after taking multiple doses of MDMA at a 48-hour rave party), the result can be the formation of a blood clot that lodges in the blood vessels that provide oxygen to the heart muscle (i.e., a heart attack) or in an artery that provides blood supply to the brain (called **ischemic stroke**). The prolonged hypertension caused by MDMA use can weaken the walls of blood vessels, which can potentially result in a rupture of the blood vessel (called a **hemorrhage**). If the rupture of one of these vessels occurs in the brain, the result could be a potentially fatal **hemorrhagic stroke**.[10]

A peculiar side effect of MDMA is frequent clenching of the jaw muscles (called **trismus**) and grinding of the teeth (called **bruxism**). Some Ecstasy users not only grind their teeth but also chew the inside of the cheek, which can result in tissue damage and open sores (**ulcerations**). The trismus and bruxism caused by MDMA is believed to be a result of the drug disturbing the chemical signaling of the nerve cells located within the brainstem that control the jaw muscles. As a result of hours of jaw and teeth clenching, Ecstasy users may later have sore jaw muscles, difficulty opening their mouths all the way, or find their teeth to be overly sensitive. Chronic Ecstasy users may show signs of dental erosion and gum inflammation due to reduced saliva production and dry mouth.[11] At many raves, Ecstasy users can be observed chewing on pacifiers or other rubber mouthpieces in order to lessen the effect of trismus and bruxism.

One of the most prominent and dangerous effects of Ecstasy is its ability to significantly increase body temperature, known as hyperthermia or **hyperpyrexia**.[12] The normal body temperature of a human being averages about 98.6 degrees Fahrenheit. Even moderate doses of MDMA can increase body temperatures by three to four degrees, similar to that of a fever caused by the flu. These increases in body temperatures can occur in any setting where the drug is taken, but are made worse by the fact that Ecstasy is often taken in the hot and crowded conditions of a rave party. In addition, prolonged physical activity such as dancing for long periods of time also worsens the hyperthermia. Increases in body temperature of two to three degrees may cause muscle aches, fatigue, chills, and headaches. The combinations of high doses of MDMA, prolonged physical activity, and hot environments in which the drug is taken can cause body temperatures to increase above a certain level (approximately 103 degrees Fahrenheit) at which severe health consequences can occur. These include seizures, severe dehydration, coma, and even death. Several studies have reported that people who were admitted to emergency rooms due to Ecstasy overdose have had body temperatures ranging from 103–110 degrees Fahrenheit, and that there is a positive correlation between the degree of hyperthermia and the likelihood of death.[13] The vast majority of people whose body temperatures surpass 108 degrees Fahrenheit end up in a coma or die. MDMA is believed to cause hyperthermia by disrupting the chemical signaling of neurons in regions of the brain (such as the hypothalamus) that regulate body temperature, as well as the chemical signaling involved in regulating heat loss such as dilation of blood vessels.[14] Because hyperthermia is very common among Ecstasy users, rave organizers often will have "cooling rooms" located within the rave location where partygoers can cool off with the help of fans, air conditioning, ice packs, and cold water. **Hyperventilation**, or increased rate of breathing, and sweating are other ways the body tries to cool itself, but this is rarely effective enough to offset the sharp increases in body temperatures produced by Ecstasy. Normally, an ice bath or packing the body with ice packs is needed to alleviate severe hyperthermia associated with MDMA use.

Ecstasy also causes the user to lose water content in the body (called **dehydration**). Several factors contribute to the ability of Ecstasy to cause dehydration—hyperthermia, excessive sweating, the ability of Ecstasy to cause the brain to release hormones that decrease water retention by the kidneys, and drinking alcohol beverages, which are diuretics and cause excess urination. Since dehydration is common among Ecstasy users, rave goers have adopted the strategy of "loading up" on water and drinking substantial quantities of it prior to going to a rave in order to prevent dehydration.[15] In addition, many raves have "water stations" set up where thirsty partygoers can rehydrate themselves by drinking cold water and reduce their hyperthermia as well. However, drinking too much water can result in a condition known as **hyponatremia**, where the levels of sodium and other electrolytes in the blood become imbalanced because of excess water drinking. Mild symptoms of hyponatremia include nausea, vomiting, and headaches, whereas more severe symptoms include seizures, coma, and swelling of the brain (called **cerebral edema**). Hyponatremia is usually treated with intravenous administration of saline at a hospital or emergency room to restore the body's natural electrolyte balance.

Another severe effect that Ecstasy use has on the kidneys is a condition called **rhabdomyolysis**. Because Ecstasy is a stimulant and users of the drug engage in long bouts of physical activity such as dancing, Ecstasy causes a breakdown of muscle tissue, which releases various muscle proteins such as **myoglobin** that enter the circulatory system and eventually lodge themselves in the kidney, resulting in potentially fatal kidney failure.[16] Myoglobin is also broken down into molecules that are harmful to the kidneys. Another manner in which Ecstasy can cause rhabdomyolysis is during acute MDMA toxicity when hyperthermia, seizures, or prolonged shaking or chills occur. Rhabdomyolysis is also observed in people who abuse other stimulants such as cocaine and methamphetamine, and is often treated by filtering of the blood by artificial kidney dialysis.

A well-known cluster of conditions that occurs with the use of Ecstasy is called the **serotonin syndrome**.[17] Its symptoms include a rapid onset of aggravation, confusion, hyperactivity, excessive sweating, unstable eye movement patterns (called **nystagmus**), irregular heart beat patterns (called **cardiac arrhythmias**), shivering, trembling, and involuntary muscle spasms and contractions that can resemble seizures. Serotonin syndrome gets its name because it is a result of the chemical actions of MDMA on synaptic terminals, where it depletes the levels of serotonin from synaptic terminals and causes an accumulation of serotonin in the synapses of the brain. MDMA also inhibits the activity of the enzyme **tryptophan hydroxylase**, which is critical for producing serotonin.[18] Thus, not only are serotonin-containing synaptic terminals depleted of their supply of this neurotransmitter, but the actions of MDMA also inhibit the production of more serotonin to replace the loss. MDMA is a frequent cause of the serotonin syndrome, but can also be a result of use of other amphetamines or by an incompatible combination of certain types of antidepressant medications. Approximately 10 to 15 percent of people who exhibit severe symptoms of serotonin syndrome die as a result.

There are numerous other physiological and unhealthy effects of Ecstasy use. Many times the all-night dancing, physical activity, lack of eating, and dehydration brought on by Ecstasy use results in complete physical exhaustion and collapse.[19] The prolonged (i.e., greater than 24 hours) physical activity and long half-lives of MDMA and MDA disrupt the normal human sleep-wake cycle, and Ecstasy users often complain of insomnia or poor sleep quality that persist long after taking the drug.[20] Repeated taking of MDMA can cause the liver to become damaged or function improperly (called **hepatitis**).[21]

Occasionally, an Ecstasy user may vomit and portions of the stomach contents enter the airways and lungs, and the result of stomach acid entering the lungs causes tiny ruptures in the air passages deep within the lungs, which result in pockets of air escaping outside the lung and becoming trapped between the lungs and the walls of the chest cavity. This condition, known as **pneumomediastinum**, has been reported to occur following Ecstasy use.[22] There have also been cases of deafness reported following Ecstasy use that were not a result of prolonged exposure to loud music, but rather neurological damage to the ear caused by Ecstasy.[23]

While physiological effects of MDMA itself can be harmful or even fatal, use of the drug can also result in dangerous and risky behaviors. For example, since rave parties are often held in large buildings or warehouses that are distant from the residences of rave attendees, injurious or fatal car accidents have been reported when rave goers have driven home while still under the influence of the drug.[24] Because of MDMA's intoxicating effects, deaths can occur as a result of falling from a second- or third-story balcony, or falling into a swimming pool and drowning. Ecstasy use can, in some cases, cause aggression and poor judgment that escalate into fights and occasionally homicide. Finally, the depression caused by a negative experience with Ecstasy can result in suicide.[25]

Ecstasy is often used in combination with other drugs such as alcohol, marijuana, or stimulants such as cocaine or methamphetamine, which can increase the likelihood of acute MDMA toxicity occurring as well as engagement in risky or harmful behaviors. Similarly, the almost indiscriminate "love" producing effects of Ecstasy may result in unprotected sex and the spread of sexually transmitted diseases.[26]

LONG-TERM EFFECTS OF ECSTASY USE

Although Ecstasy was once regarded as a "safe" and "fun" drug to use, it is now apparent that in addition to problems associated with acute MDMA toxicity long-term use of the drug can cause deficits in mental function and possible damage to the brain. These deficits in mental function include impairments in verbal and visual learning and memory, information processing, problem solving, attention and concentration, decision-making, and impulse control.[27] In addition, heavy Ecstasy users are also more prone to suffer from psychiatric

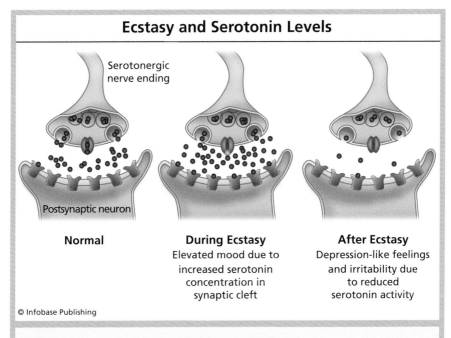

Ecstasy and Serotonin Levels

Serotonergic
nerve ending

Postsynaptic neuron

Normal

During Ecstasy
Elevated mood due to
increased serotonin
concentration in
synaptic cleft

After Ecstasy
Depression-like feelings
and irritability due
to reduced
serotonin activity

© Infobase Publishing

Figure 3.4 During normal serotonin transmission, only a small amount of serotonin is released from one neuron to the next. During Ecstasy use, a large amount of serotonin is released and the neurons become overstimulated. After taking Ecstasy, the neurons that release serotonin are often depleted of this crucial neurotransmitter. This creates a shortage of serotonin, which may cause the depression that often sets in after Ecstasy use.

problems such as psychosis, depression, anxiety, panic attacks, and other substance abuse problems, particularly when Ecstasy is used in combination with other drugs.[28] Some of these psychological problems can persist after years of abstinence from Ecstasy, whereas other mental function can recover over time in former Ecstasy users.[29] Some Ecstasy users experience frightnening **flashbacks** months after taking Ecstasy, such as visual hallucinations and feelings of reliving previous negative experiences.[30] In addition, as with most abused drugs, repeated use of a particular drug results in **tolerance** to its effects (i.e., the effects of the same dose of the drug diminish over time and the user has to increase the dose to achieve the same desired effects).[31] Tolerance is one of the criteria used when determining whether or not a person has a chemical addiction.

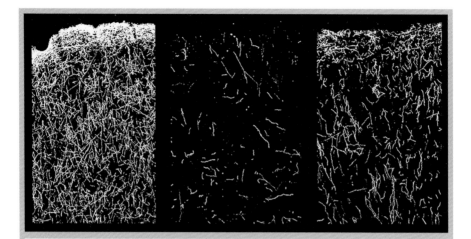

Figure 3.5 This picture shows the presence of serotonin in monkey brain neuron fibers. On the left is a normal, untreated monkey brain. The middle picture shows a similar area of brain tissues, two weeks after Ecstasy treatment. Notice the dramatic loss of serotonin-containing fibers. The picture on the right was from a monkey treated seven years earlier with Ecstasy. Serotonin-containing fibers are still reduced in these brain sections. *(National Institute on Drug Abuse)*

Most scientists believe that the cognitive and psychological problems associated with repeated use of Ecstasy are a result of direct toxic effect of MDMA on neurons that use the neurotransmitter serotonin.[32] This is known as **serotonergic neurotoxicity**, and so far it appears that MDMA is not toxic to neurons that use other neurotransmitters. Some scientists, however, speculate that the toxic effects of MDMA on the brain are due to toxic metabolites of MDMA.[33] In laboratory rats and monkeys, repeated administration of MDMA reduces the number of serotonin-containing neurons in numerous regions of the brain, notably the cerebral cortex (where thinking, planning and information processing occur [see Table 3.1]) and the hippocampus (one of the brain memory centers).[34] Similarly, studies using positron emission tomography (PET) scanning have shown that human Ecstasy users have fewer serotonin-containing synaptic terminals than non-Ecstasy users.[35] In one post-mortem study of a brain from a heavy Ecstasy user, 50 to 80 percent reductions in the levels of serotonin were found in several brain regions.[36] However, because Ecstasy is commonly used in combination with other drugs such as alcohol, marijuana, and amphetamines, it often difficult to rule out a possible role of these other abused substances in the neurotoxicity observed in Ecstasy users.

The findings illustrated in Figure 3.5 show that MDMA produces profound serotonergic neurotoxicity in the weeks immediately following repeated MDMA exposure, but years later there is some evidence of regrowth of these neurons. These findings parallel results from studies of human Ecstasy users, who show loss of serotonin neurons and cognitive impairments after heavy Ecstasy use, which can partially reverse over a period of months or years.[37]

SUMMARY

MDMA exerts its effects in the brain by causing a massive outpouring of serotonin from synaptic terminals as well as blocking the transport of serotonin back into the synaptic terminal. Serotonin-containing neurons are distributed widely throughout the brain. MDMA has a half-life of approximately nine hours, but is broken down into numerous amphetamine-related molecules such as MDA which can also contribute to some of its effects. The psychological effects of Ecstasy include euphoria, empathogenesis, entactogenesis, reductions in fears or concerns, and mild hallucinations including intensification of the senses. Not all people have positive experiences after taking Ecstasy, and some users may feel nauseous or vomit, or may become depressed, anxious, and irritable. These unpleasant symptoms are similar to those that occur after the intoxicating effects of Ecstasy wear off. Ecstasy can cause acute MDMA toxicity characterized by potential harmful or fatal hyperthermia, hypertension, dehydration, kidney failure, hepatitis, heart attacks, or strokes. Other physiological effects of Ecstasy include dilated pupils, excessive sweating, and teeth and jaw clenching. Ecstasy-induced deaths are most commonly caused by severe hyperthermia, but may also be caused by driving while under the influence of the drug, falling from balconies, drowning in pools, homicide, or suicide. Long-term Ecstasy use causes serotonin-containing nerve cells in the brain to degenerate, which can lead to numerous psychological and psychiatric problems including depression, anxiety, panic attacks, memory loss, loss of certain mental functions, and flashbacks.

4
Is Ecstasy Addictive?

Alex was the son of a violent alcoholic father. Alex started experimenting with Ecstasy at the age of 17. He started off by taking a few Ecstasy pills at high school parties on the weekends. After graduating from high school at the age of 18, he decided not to go to college but rather start a nightclub promotion business, which quickly turned very successful in the busy nightlife of downtown Atlanta, Georgia. Over time, he steadily increased his Ecstasy intake to between five and 10 pills per weekend. Because of his exposure to the nightclub scene and the numerous drugs that are used in this environment, Alex started to experiment with different types of drugs, and began to snort amphetamine regularly. Eventually Alex would start taking amphetamine and Ecstasy on Thursday nights and repeatedly take them until Monday morning, and often stayed awake almost continuously during these 80-hour weekends. Alex would spend most of Monday through Thursday recovering from these weekends, and often felt especially weak and depressed on Wednesdays, which he called the "mid-week blues." By the time Alex was 19, he spent all of his disposable income on Ecstasy and amphetamine, and began to experience significant weight loss. He also began to use cocaine and alcohol and smoke marijuana and cigarettes daily to alleviate the depression he often experienced after his weekend binges, and he sometimes would take Ecstasy to relieve his depression. Alex eventually got to the point where his work as a nightclub promoter and time off were both filled with constant drug use. While Alex knew his drug use had become excessive and could potentially harm him physically and mentally, he was unable to curb his own drug use. One Friday night after taking between 20 to 40 Ecstasy pills and a gram of amphetamine in a 24-hour period, Alex suffered a seizure, collapsing to the ground and experiencing convulsions in his arms, legs, and facial muscles. The seizure lasted only a few minutes, but with increasing concerns about Alex's health, one of his friends convinced him to go to the hospital after the seizure. The hospital staff referred Alex to a psychiatrist who specialized in substance abuse problems. During the course of interviewing Alex, the psychiatrist discovered that Alex displayed a great deal of impulsivity, had very short-lived relationships with women, and frequently needed prescription-strength sleeping pills (which he obtained through his many connections in the nightclub business) in order to sleep. Despite the seizure, Alex continued to use Ecstasy and amphetamines. The psychiatrist commenced weekly psychotherapy sessions and recommended that Alex undergo significant lifestyle changes. Realizing his drug use could potentially be life threatening, Alex got out of the nightclub business and changed to a daytime job, and was eventually able to stop using Ecstasy, amphetamine, cocaine, and sleeping pills. He was also able to curb, but not completely stop, his use of alcohol, and his daily smoking of marijuana and cigarettes continued.

This description of Alex is based on a true story reported in the medical journal *Drug and Alcohol Dependence* in 1999. There is little debate today as to whether "harder" drugs like cocaine, heroin, or methamphetamine are addictive, and it is clear that legal drugs such as alcohol and cigarettes or other nicotine-containing tobacco products are also addictive. However, whether or not Ecstasy is actually addictive has been hotly debated since its recreational use became popular in the 1970s and 1980s. Renowned psychedelic self-tester Dr. Alexander Shuglin wrote in 1986 that "MDMA does not lend itself to overuse, because its most desirable effects diminish with frequency of use."[1] Similar arguments have been made about the lack of addictive potential of other hallucinogens such as LSD or mescaline. As recently as 2001, renowned pharmacologist Dr. Harold Kalant of the University of Toronto wrote that "there is no evidence at present to suggest that MDMA or MDEA are likely to give rise to a major problem of dependence as defined in the *Diagnostic and*

Statistical Manual of Mental Disorders or the *International Statistical Classification of Diseases*."[2] However, more recent in-depth analyses of the patterns and effects of Ecstasy use have revealed that indeed Ecstasy does have the potential to be addictive and habit forming, as illustrated in the anecdote about Alex above and in the remainder of this chapter.

FACTORS THAT LEAD TO THE INITIATION OF ECSTASY USE

Most people first try Ecstasy out of curiosity about its effects, especially when they have Ecstasy- or other drug-using friends who have described their enthusiasm for Ecstasy's ability to produce intense euphoria and feelings of love, empathy, and being connected with others, according to a survey of Dutch Ecstasy users that was published by Dr. Gjalt-Jorn Peters in 2008. Other research (including a survey of 106 Dutch Ecstasy users, a survey of over 5,000 adolescent Ecstasy users in the United States, and a survey of 200 Taiwanese Ecstasy users) has found that having peers who use Ecstasy may instigate use. People who have a "thrill-" or "sensation-seeking" personality are also apt to initiate Ecstasy use. Oftentimes, first-time users will be nervous about experiencing some of the negative and toxic effects of the drug, but peer pressure or waiting until they feel more secure about having a positive experience on the drug may eventually lead them to try it. Indeed, people who are offered Ecstasy and turn down the opportunity do so out of fear of the negative effects or concern of developing an addiction to the drug.[3]

FACTORS THAT LEAD TO THE CONTINUATION OF ECSTASY USE

Some people continue using Ecstasy to experience the effects of the drug, but others may continue to use due to peer pressure and despite having the knowledge of the potential physical and psychological problems it can cause. Many Ecstasy users feel they are "immune" to these effects or are very unlikely to experience them. In addition, Ecstasy users tend to believe they can control whether or not they experience some of the potential physical dangers of Ecstasy, particularly hyperthermia and dehydration, by using **harm reduction** strategies. Such strategies include drinking large quantities of water prior to attending a rave or party where Ecstasy will be used. Many Ecstasy users dislike drinking water while under the influence of the drug, or may merely forget to do so. Some users drink alcoholic beverages or energy drinks while using Ecstasy under the false impression that this will keep them hydrated (these types of drinks are actually **diuretics**, which increase urination and increase the dehydrating effects of Ecstasy). Another harm reduction strategy is visiting cooling rooms (sometimes called "chill outs") to counteract the hyperthermic effects of Ecstasy. Other harm reduction strategies include eating healthy portions of foods prior to use (since most foods do not taste very good while under the influence of Ecstasy because the drug can produce dry mouth, and the fact that Ecstasy suppresses appetite). Some users plan on getting plenty of sleep before and after taking the drug.[4]

FACTORS THAT LEAD TO SELF-IMPOSED CESSATION OF ECSTASY USE

According to the survey by Peters and colleagues, Ecstasy users may choose to discontinue drug use, and do so for three main reasons: placing a higher priority on responsibilities such as attendance and performance at work and school, entering a relationship with another person, or starting a family. Ecstasy users can also lose interest in the drug over time. Finally, experiencing some of the negative effects of Ecstasy, such as having to be admitted to a hospital emergency room due to extreme hyperthermia, are often strong motivators for stopping Ecstasy use. Knowledge of health consequences and potential cognitive problems that are associated with long-term Ecstasy intake does not seem to be a factor in causing cessation of Ecstasy usage, since many users dismiss these effects as a result of "misuse" or "ignorance" on the part of other users, or the result of a contaminated or "bad" pill.[5]

ABUSE AND ADDICTION

The terms **substance abuse** and **substance dependence** are often used interchangeably. However, the American Psychiatric Association's *Diagnostic and Statistical Manual of Mental Disorders, Fourth Edition* (DSM-IV) makes a clear distinction between the two terms. Substance abuse is a pattern of drug use that leads to impairments in social, occupational, or academic functioning and is demonstrated by one or more of the following occurring within a 12-month period:

- repeated use of a substance results in impairments or inability to function socially, occupationally, or academically
- repeated use of a substance in physically hazardous situations (i.e., driving while intoxicated)
- repeated use of a substance resulting in legal problems (i.e., arrests for public drunkenness)
- continued use of a substance despite it causing recurrent social or interpersonal problems

Substance abuse almost always precedes the development of substance dependence, and the DSM-IV specifies that the two cannot occur in the same person at the same time.

Substance dependence—addiction—is a pattern of substance use that results in significant psychological and emotional distress, and impairment in a person's social, occupational, or academic functioning.[6] In order to meet the criteria for a diagnosis of substance dependence, a person must show at least three of the following symptoms or behaviors within a 12-month period:

1. **Tolerance** to the effect of a given drug, characterized by increasing amounts of the drug being needed to produce the desired effect, or repeated taking of the same dose of the drug resulting in diminished psychological or physiological effects.
2. The emergence of symptoms of **withdrawal** after discontinuing usage of the drug. Many addictive drugs produce a cluster of withdrawal symptoms when a person who has taken the drug repeatedly suddenly stops taking it, and these symptoms can vary by the drug that was being used. For example, withdrawal from stimulants such as cocaine, methamphetamine, or Ecstasy is characterized by feelings of depression, anxiety, irritability, fatigue but inability to sleep, and generally feeling "lousy." Withdrawal from heroin also produces irritability, insomnia, and feeling lousy, but also produces cold and clammy skin, goose bumps, diarrhea, abdominal cramps, nausea, and vomiting. For

many people, withdrawal symptoms create cravings for the drug, and as a result the addict becomes highly motivated to take the drug again to relieve the extreme discomfort of the withdrawal symptoms.

3. The drug is often taken in larger amounts or over a longer period of time than originally intended. For example, a rave partygoer might intend on just taking one or two Ecstasy pills at the beginning of a rave, but hours into the rave the effects of the drug may start to wear off and the user wishes to continue to experience its effects, so he or she ingests two more tablets. This cycle may repeat itself numerous times during a rave that lasts several days, despite the original intent of taking just one or two pills at the beginning of the rave.

4. There is a persistent desire to cut down or abstain from using the drug, and attempts at reducing or stopping drug use are most often unsuccessful. The resumption of drug taking after trying to abstain is known as **relapse**.

5. A great deal of time is spent in trying to obtain, use, and recover from the effects of drug. For example, it often takes several days to recover from repeated Ecstasy use at a weekend-long rave.

6. Drug use leads to reduced involvement in normal and important social, occupational, academic, or recreational activities. For example, a regular Ecstasy user may feel so exhausted and miserable after repeated use of the drug at a weekend-long rave that he or she is unable to report to work or school on the following Monday and Tuesday.

7. The use of the drug is continued despite the user knowing that its use might lead to serious psychological, medical, legal, social, or financial problems.

In applying these criteria to Alex, the heavy Ecstasy user mentioned at the beginning of this chapter, it is clear that he meets at least three of them, and could therefore be diagnosed as being dependent on or addicted to Ecstasy and other drugs. For example, the amount of Ecstasy Alex took per week started with just a few pills at weekend parties and eventually increased to the 20 to 40 pills he took the night he experienced a seizure, which satisfies the tolerance aspect of addiction criteria. Alex also resorted to Ecstasy and other drugs to cope with the post-Ecstasy depression and insomnia he experienced after weekend use, which satisfies the withdrawal aspect of the criteria. Alex was also unable to cut down on his use of Ecstasy and other drugs, and continued taking Ecstasy despite having a seizure.

DO SOME ECSTASY USERS MEET THE CRITERIA FOR ADDICTION?

Despite the assertions by Drs. Shulgin and Kalant that Ecstasy poses little or no risk for addiction, there is accumulating evidence that repeated, heavy use of Ecstasy can result in psychological and physical dependence on the drug as well as other abused substances. The following research reports support this evidence.

In 2001, Dr. Linda Cottler and her colleagues at Washington University in St. Louis reported results of their examination of 52 young adults in the city of St. Louis, Missouri, who frequented night clubs and used drugs regularly. This report showed that 43 percent of these individuals met the DSM-IV criteria for dependence on Ecstasy, and that 34 percent met the criteria for Ecstasy abuse.[7]

Dr. Cottler subsequently expanded on her previous findings by studying the incidence of Ecstasy dependence and abuse in almost 600 users from St. Louis, Miami, and Sydney, Australia. Dr. Cottler found that 59 percent of these users met the criteria for Ecstasy dependence, and 15 percent met the criteria for Ecstasy abuse. Symptoms most frequently reported were continued use despite knowledge of potential health problems (Criteria 7) and the presence of withdrawal symptoms (Criteria 2). Dr. Cottler's study also suggested that Ecstasy-dependent persons may not necessarily need to be classified as simply "dependent" or "not dependent" on the drug, but that Ecstasy dependence should be subcategorized as "mild," "moderate," or "severe," depending on the number of symptoms experienced.[8]

In 2007, Drs. Cheng-Fang Yen and Sen-Yen Hsu of Kaoshiung Medical University in Taiwan reported on their research findings of 200 Taiwanese Ecstasy users. They found that 37 percent of these Ecstasy users reported continued use despite knowledge of potential health problems, 29.5 percent reported that they spent a great deal of time obtaining the drug or recovering from its effects, and 23.5 percent reported that they experience tolerance to the effects of Ecstasy. This report indicates that roughly one-third of these Taiwanese Ecstasy users could be diagnosed as being dependent on Ecstasy.[9]

A group of researchers led by Dr. James Anthony at the University of Washington in Seattle found that Ecstasy users were significantly more likely to become dependent on the drug, as defined by the DSM-IV criteria, than those who used LSD.[10]

In a survey of more than 55,000 adolescent Ecstasy users age 12–17, Dr. Li-Tzy Wu and colleagues at Duke University reported that 38.5 percent showed symptoms of Ecstasy abuse or dependence, and that these adolescents most often reported tolerance to the effects of Ecstasy (Criteria 1), increased time spent obtaining or recovering from the effects of Ecstasy (Criteria 5), and continued use despite knowledge of problems (Criteria 7).[11]

Finally, in a survey of 59 current and former Ecstasy users in Germany who had taken approximately 800 Ecstasy tablets in their lifetime, Dr. R. Thomasius and colleagues reported that 73 percent of these individuals could either currently or previously be diagnosed as being dependent on Ecstasy.[12]

These recent studies suggest that, despite early assertions to the contrary, Ecstasy can indeed be addictive in some users. Numerous factors contribute to the development of Ecstasy addiction, including peer pressure to continue drug use and combined use of Ecstasy with other drugs. Heavy use of Ecstasy and dependence on the drug is associated with higher levels of cognitive difficulties such as memory problems and problem solving, which is likely a result of increased serotonergic neurotoxicity caused by the drug.[13]

IS ECSTASY A "GATEWAY" TO USING OTHER DRUGS?

Ecstasy users tend to have more problems with use of other substances such as alcohol, cigarettes, marijuana, cocaine, heroin, and methamphetamine than do users of other hallucinogens such as LSD or people who do not use hallucinogens at all. This has led many researchers, and the public at large, to wonder whether Ecstasy increases the risk of using and becoming addicted to other drugs. In other words, some people feel that Ecstasy opens a "gateway" to using "harder" drugs such as cocaine, heroin, or methamphetamime. This is sometimes referred to as the **gateway theory**, and has been speculated to occur not only in users of Ecstasy but marijuana as well. There is some evidence to support this theory. In a survey of more than 54,000 people, Dr. Silvia Martins of the Johns Hopkins Bloomberg School of Public Health found

Figure 4.1 There is some evidence to suggest that Ecstasy is a gateway drug, meaning that those who use it may be more likely to use other "harder" drugs such as cocaine or heroin. *(Shutterstock)*

that use of Ecstasy is more likely to lead to use of other "harder" drugs such as cocaine or heroin than in people who do not use Ecstasy. However, the issue is more complicated than it may first appear. For example, according by a study by Dr. Lesley Reid, individuals who initiate Ecstasy use later in adolescence (i.e., at approximately age 18) are actually *less* likely to later initiate the use of cocaine and methamphetamine than those who initiate Ecstasy use earlier in adolescence (i.e., at age 14 or 15). In addition, some other drugs may also be "gateway" drugs to Ecstasy use. For example, it has been shown that marijuana may be a gateway drug that predicts future use of Ecstasy. While use of Ecstasy is well known to be associated with higher use rates of "harder" drugs, many other factors may alter the trajectory future drug use, such as age at which Ecstasy use is initiated, use of marijuana, access to other drugs, having money to purchase such drugs, peer pressure, etc. Thus, with these many other possible contributing factors, the gateway theory of Ecstasy use leading to harder drug use is difficult to prove as fact.[14]

SUMMARY

Over the last decade, a substantial amount of evidence has accumulated showing that, in some individuals, repeated use of Ecstasy may lead to abuse of or dependence on the drug, which increases the likelihood of developing Ecstasy-induced psychological problems and serotonergic neurotoxicity. Ecstasy use is often associated with use of other "harder" drugs such as cocaine, methamphetamine, and heroin, and is therefore often thought of as a "gateway" drug that can lead to future drug-related problems, though many other factors can also contribute to future drug use. In the next chapter, factors that lead to repeated Ecstasy use will be discussed, as will strategies to prevent Ecstasy use and abuse and ways to treat addiction to Ecstasy.

5

Prevention and Treatment of Ecstasy Abuse and Addiction

Carl was a 25 year-old electrical repairman with a history of psychological problems when he first came to a substance abuse clinic. His father had been an alcoholic, and Carl underwent frequent psychological counseling as a child for temper control problems. At the age of 16, Carl left home to move in with his girlfriend Janice who had also run away from a dysfunctional family. He fathered two children with Janice, but she subsequently ended the relationship and retained custody of the children. When Carl was 24, as part of his job as an electrician, he was hired to install a series of lighting fixtures at the home of a couple undergoing a bitter divorce. On the third day working at their home, the estranged husband (after learning his wife was going to be entitled to keep their upscale residence) burst into the house brandishing a shotgun and yelled "Where is she?!? I'm gonna kill her!" At that particular moment, Carl was working in the downstairs kitchen and was paralyzed by fear when he saw the man burst into the house with a gun. The man proceeded up the stairs to find his wife and shot her twice before turning the gun on himself. In the months following the murder-suicide, Carl began to experience extreme feelings of guilt for not having tried to interve to save the woman's life. He also started to experience insomnia, low appetite and weight loss, low energy levels, a loss of interest in life, and feelings of depression, anxiety, and being detached from others. Carl also had occasional suicidal thoughts and frequent nightmares and flashbacks about the crime (these symptoms are frequently exhibited by people who have witnessed or experienced an *extremely traumatic event, and the disorder is called **post-traumatic stress disorder**, or **PTSD**). To rid himself of these feelings, Carl became a frequent and heavy alcohol drinker at a bar that was in walking distance of his apartment. One night at the bar, someone offered him an Ecstasy pill, which he took. Within the next several hours Carl's mood dramatically increased and he began to feel "reconnected" with the world and the people who surrounded him. Having been lifted out of the state of depression and isolation that he had been trapped within since witnessing the murder-suicide, Carl's use of Ecstasy increased steadily over the next few months, and two years after his initial Ecstasy experience, he was taking 25 to 30 tablets per weekend. He even sold many of his possessions, such as his television and clothes, in order to purchase Ecstasy. Carl's use of alcohol also escalated, drinking an entire bottle of whiskey almost every night, and he smoked a pack of cigarettes every day. Carl's mother, who had witnessed his decline in health and mental well-being that paralleled his heavy use of drugs, eventually convinced Carl to see a psychiatrist who specialized in substance abuse in patients with PTSD. Through extensive psychiatric help Carl was able to eventually completely abstain from Ecstasy use and cut down on his alcohol use. Carl's psychiatrist also prescribed an antidepressant medication to improve his symptoms of depression and anxiety, which helped improve Carl's overall mental well-being. Carl was then able to resume work as an electrician and soon started a serious relationship with a woman.*

The preceding passage is based on a true case study.[1] It clearly demonstrates how the use of Ecstasy, whether initiated for pleasure or to remove psychological pain, can lead to a downward spiral into addiction and mental instability. In this chapter, common approaches for preventing Ecstasy use and abuse will be discussed, as will strategies for treating addiction to Ecstasy.

PREVENTION AND HARM REDUCTION

There is an old saying used by addicts and those who treat them: "The best way to quit taking drugs is to never start." There is a lot of truth in this saying, because addiction to drugs is one of the most difficult psychiatric disorders to treat. Drugs produce numerous long-lasting changes in the brain. Many government and nonprofit organizations focus a lot of effort on educating the public about drugs, the potential harm that they cause to the brain and body, and the tremendous toll they take on the addict's families, educational and occupational performance, health care and legal costs to society, and individual financial stability. Educational and other measures have been developed to prevent or reduce Ecstasy use and addiction to Ecstasy.

EDUCATIONAL OUTREACH EFFORTS TO PREVENT INITIATION OF ECSTASY USE

The use of Ecstasy by teenagers surged dramatically between 1999 and 2002 by about 71 percent, surpassing the use of cocaine, heroin, and methamphetamine by this same age group. In response to this dramatic increase in Ecstasy use, the nonprofit organization Partnership for a Drug-Free America launched one of the first educational campaigns specifically targeting the use of Ecstasy. This campaign was not only designed to educate teenagers about the risks of Ecstasy use, but also to increase the awareness of parents about Ecstasy. This campaign used multiple media approaches to spread the organization's message about Ecstasy, including TV advertisements, magazine and newspaper ads, educational pamphlets, and video testimonials from former Ecstasy users whose lives were dramatically disrupted by Ecstasy use. The campaign lasted two years and cost at least $30 million in media exposure. This aggressive campaign appeared to be effective, as the year 2003 witnessed a 25 percent drop in Ecstasy use among teenagers as compared to 2001.

Not all educational efforts at reducing the problems associated with Ecstasy come from organizations that promote complete abstinence from the drug. For example, one of the primary efforts of the organization DanceSafe is to educate Ecstasy users about the potential harmful effects of the drug and reduce the incidences of Ecstasy-related health problems by harm reduction and tablet testing.[2] The organization's Web site is filled with tips on the "safe" use of MDMA, such as promoting drinking water to staying hydrated and avoiding hyperthermia by visiting cooling rooms at raves. The organization also offers free testing of Ecstasy tablets submitted by mail, and even sells home testing kits similar to those used at raves to determine the content of

WHAT'S IN THAT PILL?
ECSTASY TABLET CONTENT TESTING

Occasionally, Ecstasy sellers and users may wish to have the purity of MDMA in their tablets tested. This can be done by private companies using sophisticated chemical analysis techniques, but each test typically costs $100 or more. Other "on-the-spot" chemical tests can be performed for far less money at booths set up at raves. During these tests, part of an Ecstasy tablet is scraped off into a white ceramic dish and mixed with a specific chemical, the product of which turns a certain color. The color of the chemical reaction product can be compared against a color chart that indicates the presence or absence of MDMA. The first of these chemical tests was called Marquis reagent and consisted of a mixture of sulfuric acid and formaldehyde. Other tests were subsequently developed that used chemicals such as Mecke reagent (selenious acid and sulfuric acid), or Simon's reagent (sodium nitroprusside, acetaldehyde and sodium carbonate). However, these chemical tests only look for the presence or absence of MDMA in an Ecstasy tablet, not the amount of MDMA, which can vary from 30 to 200 mg per tablet, nor can they detect the presence or concentrations of contaminants such as MDEA, MDA, PMA, etc. In addition, the resulting color is subject to individual interpretation, and is often done under improper lighting conditions.[4]

Ecstasy pills. Organizations like DanceSafe assert that education about "safe" use of Ecstasy decreases the potential for addiction, and that serious health consequences only occur in "undereducated" Ecstasy users. This organization does acknowledge that addiction to Ecstasy can occur and will refer people to appropriate treatment resources when needed.

While "scare tactics" such as photographs of teenagers who have died after taking Ecstasy are an effective deterrent against its use for some, others largely ignore these warnings. Some researchers have suggested that the best form of prevention is peer-based education (i.e., fellow teens or young adults educating their peers about the potential harms of Ecstasy use), likely because teenagers and young adults tend to listen to their friends and largely ignore the advice of the parents, educators, or legal authorities.[3]

TREATMENT OF ECSTASY ADDICTION

Because the notion of addiction to Ecstasy has only recently become support-ed by scientific studies, and the fact that some believe that it is not addictive and may actually have some therapeutic value, no current therapies that have been specifically designed and proven effective for the treatment of Ecstasy addiction. There are, however, some approaches that have been used in the treatment of addiction to other substances such as cocaine, heroin, alcohol, cigarettes, and methamphetamine.

One of the most widely used approaches to treating addiction is **cognitive-behavioral therapy (CBT)**. CBT helps a person overcome his or her problems by identifying and changing abnormal or irrational think-ing, behavior, and emotional responses. In order to do so, the therapist must work closely with the patient to develop skills for modifying his or her beliefs, identifying problematic thinking patterns, relating to others in more positive ways, and changing problematic behaviors (i.e., drug use). CBT often involves keeping a diary of daily events and associated feelings, thoughts, and behav-iors. The therapist will help the patient question and test unrealistic or self-defeating beliefs, interpretations, and assumptions. The patient is encouraged to participate in activities that may have been previously avoided, and to try new ways of behaving and reacting. CBT is often used in conjunction with psychotherapeutic medications such as antidepressants or mood stabilizers, which can relieve symptoms of depression or unstable moods that lead to Ecstasy use.

In the case of someone addicted to Ecstasy, the therapist may work with the patient on improving his or her ability to refuse Ecstasy if offered, even in the face of strong pressure from peers. To avoid the temptation of taking Ecstasy, the patient may be encouraged to avoid situations in which Ecstasy is frequently used, such as raves or dance clubs.[5] In the case of Carl, the Ec-stasy addict described at the beginning of this chapter who also suffered from PTSD, the therapist would likely work intensely on alleviating the feelings of guilt and shame that Carl felt as a result of not intervening in the murder-suicide that he witnessed. An antianxiety medication might also be prescribed to alleviate Carl's anxiety and flashbacks, and he might also undergo attempts at curbing his alcohol and cigarette use.

SUMMARY

Ecstasy use is most often initiated out of curiosity to experience the drug's effects, especially among people who socialize with Ecstasy users. Peer pressure also plays a role in initiation of Ecstasy use, as do sensation-seeking personality traits. Continued use of the drug, even with the knowledge of potential harmful effects, is perpetuated by peer pressure and the misconception that people who suffer the harmful effects are using it "improperly," and are undereducated about harm-reduction strategies that can be used to defend against negative effects such as dehydration and hyperthermia. The availability of pill testing for determining the presence of MDMA in a particular Ecstasy tablet also perpetuates a feeling of safety among Ecstasy users. People who voluntarily stop using Ecstasy do so out of loss of interest in the drug's mood-lifting effects, having a negative experience with the drug, or placing a higher priority on performance at school, work, or starting a family. Ecstasy use and toxicity can also be reduced by multimedia anti-drug campaigns. Because scientific evidence for the existence of addiction to Ecstasy has only recently emerged, specific and successful programs for treatment of Ecstasy addiction have not yet been developed. Standard therapeutic approaches used to treat other addictions are therefore normally employed, such as CBT with or without psychotherapeutic medications, and treatment of underlying psychological disorders that lead to Ecstasy use.

6
Legal and Therapeutic Aspects of Ecstasy

"In terms of therapeutic potential, MDMA is remarkably effective, gentle yet profound…MDMA rarely interferes with cognitive functioning or perception and usually produces a warm, emotionally grounded feeling with a sense of self-acceptance, and a reduction of fear and defensiveness." This statement comes from an article published by Dr. Rick Doblin, president of the Multidisciplinary Association for Psychedelic Studies (MAPS), an organization established in 1986 that advocates research on the use of marijuana and psychedelics for medical purposes.[1] In 2002, MAPS initiated a 10-year, $10 million project aimed at obtaining approval by the FDA to use MDMA in conjunction with psychotherapy to heal PTSD and other traumas caused by sexual assault, war, violent crime, etc. On June 14, 2002, the FDA granted permission to Dr. Michael Mithoefer of Charleston, South Carolina, to conduct this research. The study was performed on 21 subjects with treatment-resistant PTSD as a result of sexual abuse, crime, or war, and was completed in September 2008. The results of this study have not yet been published. MAPS has also initiated research on the use of Ecstasy for the treatment of PTSD in other countries such as Spain, Israel, Jordan, Switzerland, and Canada. In addition, MAPS has recently initiated a study at Harvard Medical School's McLean Hospital to determine the effectiveness of MDMA-assisted psychotherapy in treating patients with anxiety associated with advanced-stage cancer.

One could easily argue that some of Doblin's claims quoted above are incorrect, since it is well known that Ecstasy can cause cognitive disturbances and mild hallucinations. In addition, despite Ecstasy being illegal for more than two decades, there is still a push by many psychiatrists, therapists, and organizations such as MAPS to have the drug legalized for use in conjunction with psychotherapy to treat various mental illnesses and psychological problems.[2] However, this type of research, which must be conducted in a very closely controlled and monitored manner, is usually met with strong resistance from medical doctors who have witnessed firsthand the destructive capabilities of Ecstasy, or from politicians who fear that legalization could pave the way for approval of medical use of many dangerous drugs that are currently illegal. In this chapter, recent legal efforts to increase the penalties for Ecstasy use and trafficking will be summarized, as will the arguments for and against the use of Ecstasy in psychotherapy.

RECENT ECSTASY-RELATED LEGAL MEASURES

Ecstasy was made illegal in 1986. Despite this, a dramatic surge in Ecstasy use, especially among teenagers, occurred in the late 1990s. In response to this increase in Ecstasy use, Senator Bob Graham of Florida introduced the Ecstasy Anti-Proliferation Act of 2000 (Senate Bill 2612) to the U.S. Congress on March 23, 2000, which provided stronger punishments for Ecstasy trafficking, increased education of the public about the dangers of Ecstasy, provided additional funding to the National Institute on Drug Abuse for research on Ecstasy addiction, and prohibited placing information about ways to manufacture Ecstasy on the Internet. This bill became law on November 1, 2001, and in response, the U.S. Sentencing Commission increased the punishment for trafficking MDMA. Specifically, the bill increased the sentence for trafficking up to 800 Ecstasy pills from 15 months to 5 years, and increased the penalty for trafficking up to 8,000 Ecstasy pills from 41 months to 10 years.

Following his introduction of the Ecstasy Anti-Proliferation Act of 2000, Senator Graham next introduced the Ecstasy Prevention Act of 2001 (Senate Bill 1208) to the U.S. Senate on July 19, 2001. This bill encouraged communities to ban rave events in exchange for higher priority for receiving federal

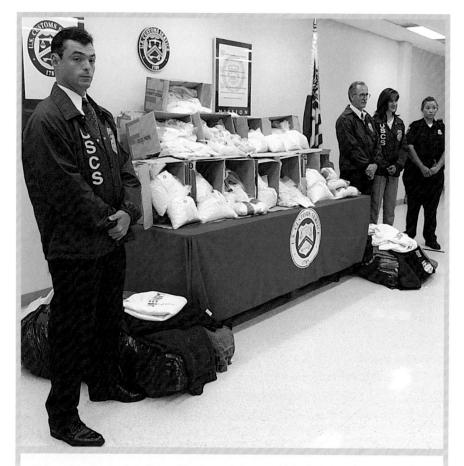

Figure 6.1 Bags of confiscated Ecstasy, guarded by Customs agents, are shown here. The punishment for trafficking Ecstasy can be quite severe, ranging from 15 months to 10 years, depending on the number of tablets seized. Possession of Ecstasy can also result in jail time, although treatment and counseling is often recommended for Ecstasy users. *(AP Images)*

grant funding. In addition, it authorized the use of $15 million to increase anti-Ecstasy law enforcement in high trafficking areas and an additional $1 million to establish a Federal Task Force on Ecstasy/MDMA and Emerging Club Drugs, which would report to the President and Congress on strategies to improve Ecstasy control. On December 20, 2001, a slightly modified version of the bill was added by amendment to House of Representatives

Bill 2215 (the 21st-Century Department of Justice Appropriations Authorization Act). The Senate then passed this bill, but the Ecstasy-control provisions of it were deleted from the final version before it was signed into law on November 2, 2002.

On June 18, 2002, Senate Bill 2633, the Reducing Americans' Vulnerability to Ecstasy Act of 2002, or RAVE Act, was introduced into the Senate. The RAVE Act would have criminalized rave parties and rave organizers on the grounds of using a specified place temporarily to profit from the use of a controlled substance. Similar bans on "crack houses" had previously been passed by Congress. However, this bill attracted a significant degree of opposition from the American Civil Liberties Union and music event and rave promoters. An estimated 500 protestors demonstrated against this bill at the U.S. Capitol Building on September 6, 2002. As a result, several members of the Senate Judiciary Committee who were original sponsors of the bill withdrew their sponsorship of the RAVE Act, and the bill was never passed.

INTERNATIONAL TRAFFICKING OF ECSTASY

In the past, the United Nations Office for Drug Control and Crime Prevention (ODCCP) has asserted that approximately 90 percent of the world's supply of Ecstasy was synthesized in illegal laboratories in Belgium and the Netherlands, which was then trafficked to the rest of the world by organized crime units. However, in recent years, there has been a shift in the source of Ecstasy coming into the United States from these European countries to its northern neighbor, Canada. As a result, the Drug Enforcement Agency (DEA) initiated Operation Candy Box, which was aimed at dismantling the illegal synthesis and trafficking of Ecstasy tablets into the United States from Canada, and eventually disrupted a drug trafficking ring that supplied one million Ecstasy tablets to the United States per month. Operation Candy Box ended in 2004, and was followed by Operation Sweet Tooth in 2005, which eventually disrupted a drug trafficking ring that supplied 1.5 million Ecstasy tablets to the United States per month. In 2006, Operation Triple Play was initiated, and according to the U.S. Office of National Drug Control Policy, a total of 5,485,619 Ecstasy pills were seized at the U.S.–Canada border that year. A common element in all of these operations

Figure 6.2   Bags of confistcated Ecstasy that were smuggled in the trunk of a car. (*U.S. Customs and Border Patrol*)

is that they resulted in the arrest of individuals with ties to Asian organized crime units.

SHOULD ECSTASY BE LEGALIZED FOR THERAPEUTIC PURPOSES?

Drs. Alexander Shulgin, George Greer, and other scientists and psychiatrists have long asserted that Ecstasy could be used for therapeutic purposes in conjunction with traditional psychotherapy. In order for Ecstasy to be used for such purposes, the DEA would have to reclassify it as a Schedule II, III, IV, or V controlled substance, since its current classification as a Schedule I drug prohibits its use for any reason. The arguments that some

IS ECSTASY A DATE RAPE DRUG?

Many club drugs, so-named for their common use at dance clubs, have been portrayed by the media as **date rape drugs**, since they have the effect of incapacitating the person who ingests it to a point that he or she is physically unable to resist unwanted sexual advances or sexual assault. Two of the most common drugs that are referred to as date rape drugs are the sedative **flunitrazepam** (Rohypnol, often called "roofies") and **gamma-hydroxybutyrate (GHB)**, a potent intoxicating substance. There is clear evidence that these drugs can indeed render a person a "helpless slave" to the sexual desires of another individual. Because Ecstasy produces feelings of love and closeness, as well as reductions in the sense of fear, Ecstasy is sometimes also labeled as a date rape drug. In support of this notion, traces of Ecstasy have been found in blood samples of date rape victims. While people who use Ecstasy are more likely to engage in risky (i.e., unprotected) sex than those who do not use it, whether Ecstasy itself is a true date rape drug is still under debate. Many experts believe that highly intoxicating doses of Ecstasy alone do not render the victim completely helpless and compliant to all sexual advances. Rather, the hyperthermia, agitation, irritability, and other behaviors associated with high doses of MDMA may allow the person to resist sexual assault. However, combining Ecstasy with sedatives such as alcohol or club drugs such as Rohypnol or GHB could potentially cause the user to become involuntarily sexually submissive.[3]

therapists use to support their position that Ecstasy is potentially beneficial when used in conjunction with psychotherapy include the following established facts about Ecstasy:[4]

- Promotes deeper contact with the self.
- Enhances recognition of positive aspects of the self and others.
- Produces more positive feelings and attitudes about life.

- Reduces fear so that a previous negative or traumatic event can be recalled without discomfort and re-evaluated by the patient and therapist.
- Promotes a strong interpersonal bond between the patient and the therapist, which increases the patient's trust in the therapist and allows him or her to be more "open" about expressing feelings.

Opponents of Ecstasy legalization cite equally numerous reasons why it should not be legalized for use in psychotherapy:

- Not everyone has a positive experience after taking Ecstasy, and some individuals experience anxiety, depression, confusion, and mental fatigue due to "racing thoughts." Negative experiences with Ecstasy occur more frequently in people who are in a negative mood state (i.e., a bad mood) prior to taking Ecstasy. In other words, Ecstasy can make some people's bad moods even worse, which would obviously not be beneficial in psychotherapy.[5]
- Ecstasy can cause the user to experience panic due to feelings of depersonalization, fear of losing control over their thoughts, and visual hallucinations.
- Ecstasy can produce fatigue, irritability, depression, nightmares, anxiety, muscle aches, and reduced appetite in the hours or days following use of the drug.
- Great care needs to be taken to ensure that patients taking Ecstasy are in the correct positive mental state, and that both the therapist and patient are in complete agreement regarding the expected outcome of the therapy session.
- Some proponents of Ecstasy-assisted psychotherapy suggest that all therapists who administer Ecstasy to their patients should understand what it feels like to be under the influence of the drug.[6] However, since there is a wide spectrum of experiences after taking Ecstasy, and the fact that the patient has a psychological disorder such as PTSD (and presumably the therapist does not), there can be no certainty about whether the therapist and patient will experience the same effects of Ecstasy.

- Unlike most approved therapeutic drugs for psychological disorders, Ecstasy cannot be taken over long periods of time without the possibility of developing long-term serotonergic neurotoxicity, impairments in cognitive function such as memory loss, addiction, and possibly the development of other psychiatric disorders.
- Even supporters of Ecstasy use in psychotherapy suggest that the drug should not be used in patients with psychological disorders known to be a result of chemical imbalances in the brain or with genetic components, but only in people who need assistance in processing difficult emotions such as post-traumatic fear and anxiety. Use of Ecstasy in people with pre-existing moderate to severe psychological problems may make them more vulnerable to a resurgence or worsening of such problems.[7]
- Questioning whether a single psychotherapy session in which Ecstasy is used is sufficient enough to produce long-lasting psychological improvements without the need for additional therapy sessions with Ecstasy.[8]

It is likely that the debate over whether the potential benefits of using Ecstasy in combination with psychotherapy outweigh the risks of taking the drug will continue for many years to come. In order to be approved for use, the increasingly strict FDA needs to be thoroughly convinced that Ecstasy can be used safely and without short-term or long-term harm under the careful supervision of a trained therapist to assist in the treatment of psychological problems and disorders.

SUMMARY

When usage of Ecstasy began to dramatically increase around the year 1999, various acts of legislation were introduced to curb the use, sale, and trafficking of the drug. the Ecstasy Anti-Proliferation Act of 2000 was approved and sharply increased the penalties for trafficking Ecstasy in the United States. The following year, the Ecstasy Prevention Act of 2001 was introduced to entice communities to ban raves and increase funding for law enforcement agencies to curb Ecstasy trafficking; however, the Ecstasy control provisions of this bill were deleted prior to it being approved. In 2002, the Reducing Americans' Vulnerability to Ecstasy Act of 2002, or RAVE Act, was introduced to criminalize raves and their organizers and essentially classify them as "crack houses" for Ecstasy use. This bill failed to become law. With regards to Ecstasy trafficking, it has been long thought that the majority of Ecstasy tablets that are sold in the United States are made in illegal laboratories in western European countries. However, there has been an increase in the production and trafficking of Ecstasy into the United States from its northern neighbor Canada. Finally, the debates over whether Ecstasy is a date rape drug or whether it can and should be used legally in psychological therapy both continue to this day.

7
Summary and Conclusions

Lynn was a straight-A student who was involved in many school activities and hung out with the "popular crowd" at her high school. Lynn had always dreamed of moving to New York to study acting and pursue a career in theater, and her dream came true when her mother brought her to New York to attend acting school. With this change in scenery, Lynn was exposed to new people, some of whom had been into drugs for many years. Lynn felt pressured to try some of these drugs like marijuana and Ecstasy in order to fit in. The first time Lynn tried Ecstasy, she felt a tremendous feeling of bliss and connection with the universe, and that she had unlocked a secret world and found heaven. Lynn eventually started to use Ecstasy more frequently. Ecstasy gave Lynn a sense of exclusivity, and she started to look down on non-Ecstasy users and only wanted to be around those who used the drug. She had gone from someone who never used drugs to someone who couldn't imagine life without them. Lynn used Ecstasy frequently at many night clubs, parties, bars, and apartments.

Eventually, her repeated use of Ecstasy resulted in a loss of interest in a career in theater, and occasionally she would go days without eating or sleeping. Lynn often reflected on her first experience with Ecstasy, and it seemed that she could never recapture those beautiful feelings no matter how much Ecstasy she took. Lynn's experiences on Ecstasy soon turned for the worst, causing her feelings of sadness, loneliness, paranoia, and she began to experience nightmares and shaking in her arms and hands. One night, Lynn had a terrifying experience while watching

75

a movie with her roommates. She suddenly started to experience rac-
ing thoughts and horrible images entering her mind. She had visions of
seeing the devil, and repeatedly asked her roommates if she was dead.
Lynn was also struck with a restless panic and felt as if she were hav-
ing a heart attack. Eventually she called her mother to come get her.
The next morning Lynn's mother took her to the psychiatric ward of
a hospital, where she stayed for the next 14 days in a state of extreme
confusion.

After being discharged from the hospital, Lynn saw many doctors
and therapists who put her on various antidepressant, antipsychotic,
and mood stabilizing medications, which helped her regain her ability
to function seminormally as a result of the chemical imbalance caused
by her long-term Ecstasy use. Lynn now worries about her future and
health every day, and blames no one but herself for having taken this
particular road to ruin. Yet she remains optimistic because she feels
she has been lucky enough to be given a second chance, which very few
people get. Today, Lynn still hears people talking about Ecstasy as a fun,
harmless drug. Each time she hears this, all she can think is "if they only
knew."

The above passage is a true story about 22-year-old Lynn Smith, who appeared on a September 2001 segment of *The Oprah Winfrey Show* titled "What Parents Should Know About Ecstasy." Lynn discussed her experiences on Ecstasy with hopes of deterring others from starting to use the drug.

In summary, Ecstasy/MDMA is an illegal hallucinogen and stimulant that is chemically related to methamphetamine. It is primarily taken by teenagers and young adults at rave parties or other social gatherings to intensify physical sensations and perceptions, increase self-esteem and sociability, and produce profound feelings of euphoria, love, and empathy. However, not everyone who takes Ecstasy has a positive experience with the drug, as some people may become depressed, anxious, or have panic attacks.

Ecstasy use is most often initiated out of curiosity to experience the drug's effects, especially among people who socialize with Ecstasy users. Peer pressure also plays a role in initiation and continuation of Ecstasy use. Another factor that perpetuates Ecstasy use is the misconception that people who suffer the harmful effects are using it improperly and are undereducated about harm reduction strategies. These strategies include taking steps to avoid the dangerous and potential fatal effects of Ecstasy such as dehydration and hyperthermia. Organiztions such as DanceSafe and RaveSafe often set up tables or booths at rave parties for free testing of Ecstasy pills to verify that they contain MDMA. However, these tests often are not designed to detect all other potential dangerous stimulants or chemicals present in the pill and may give the Ecstasy user a false sense of security about the drug.

MDMA was first chemically synthesized by German scientists in 1912 at the pharmaceutical company Merck. Despite common assertations to the contrary, MDMA was not developed as an appetite suppressant or weight loss drug. MDMA was tested by scientists and the U.S. military on animals and humans for its toxic and physiological effects in the 1950s, and the psychedelic, empathogenic, and entactogenic effects of MDMA were first reported in the 1970s. At that time, numerous scientists, psychiatrists, and psychological counselors felt that MDMA could be of great benefit to patients undergoing psychotherapy so as to break down people's fears and emotional barriers. However, MDMA began to be used recreationally during the early 1980s and because of growing fears of potential harmful effects of the drug, the DEA made MDMA illegal in 1986. Despite criminalization, recreational MDMA use continued to increase and peaked in the years 1998–2002. During this time, various pieces of legislation were introduced to curb the use, sale, and trafficking of the drug. The Ecstasy Anti-Proliferation Act of 2000 was approved and sharply increased the penalties for trafficking Ecstasy in the United States. The following year, the Ecstasy Prevention Act of 2001 was introduced to entice communities to ban raves and increase funding for law enforcement agencies to curb Ecstasy trafficking; however, the Ecstasy control provisions of this bill were deleted prior to it being approved. In 2002, the Reducing Americans' Vulnerability to Ecstasy Act of 2002, or RAVE Act, was introduced to criminalize raves and their organizers and essentially classify them as "crack houses" for Ecstasy use. This bill failed to become law. Since the peak in MDMA use in 1998–2002, MDMA use has declined but remained relatively stable in recent years, perhaps due to successful educational campaigns by antidrug organizations and publicity of deaths resulting from its use.

MDMA exerts its effects in the brain by causing a massive outpouring of serotonin from synaptic terminals as well as blocking the transport of serotonin back into the synaptic terminal. MDMA has a half-life of approximately nine hours, but it broken down into numerous amphetamine-related molecules such as MDA which can also contribute to some of its effects. While positive feelings are usually reported by first-time MDMA users, some users may feel nauseous or vomit, or may become depressed, anxious, and irritable. Ecstasy can cause acute MDMA toxicity characterized by potential harmful or fatal hyperthermia, hypertension, dehydration, kidney failure, hepatitis, heart attacks, or strokes. Other effects of Ecstasy include dilated pupils, excessive sweating, and teeth and jaw clenching. Ecstasy-induced deaths are most commonly caused by severe hyperthermia. Long-term Ecstasy use causes serotonin-containing nerve cells in the brain to degenerate, which can lead to numerous psychological and psychiatric problems including depression, anxiety, panic attacks, memory loss, loss of certain mental functions, and flashbacks.

In some individuals, repeated use of Ecstasy may lead to addiction to the drug, which increases the likelihood of developing Ecstasy-induced psychological problems. Because scientific evidence for the existence of addiction to Ecstasy has only recently emerged, specific and successful programs for treatment of Ecstasy addiction have not yet been developed. Standard therapeutic approaches that are used to treat other addictions are therefore normally employed, such as CBT with or without psychotherapeutic medications, and treatment of underlying psychological disorders that lead to Ecstasy use.

Ecstasy is often associated with use of other "harder" drugs such as cocaine, methamphetamine, and heroin, and is therefore often thought of as a "gateway" drug that can lead to future drug-related problems, though many other environmental, psychological, and genetic factors can also contribute to future drug use. The issue of legalization of Ecstasy for use in psychotherapy was initiated by Dr. Alexander Shulgin, the "Father of Ecstasy," in the 1980s, and has continued for the last quarter century.

Appendix

Classification of Controlled Substances

In 1970, the U.S. government passed the Controlled Substances Act, which classified all drugs into one of five categories, or "schedules." In effect, this law classified drugs and other substances according to how medically useful, safe, and potentially addictive they are. These schedules are defined as follows:

Schedule I—The drug has (1) a high potential for abuse, (2) no currently accepted medical use in the United States, and (3) a lack of accepted safety. Ecstasy is classified as a Schedule I substance, as are marijuana, heroin, psilocybin, LSD, and other hallucinogens such as peyote and mescaline.

Schedule II—(1) The drug has a high potential for abuse, (2) the drug has a currently accepted medical use in the United States or a currently accepted medical use with severe restrictions, and (3) abuse of the drug may lead to severe psychological or physical dependence. Cocaine, morphine, methamphetamine, and d-amphetamine are examples of Schedule II substances.

Schedule III—(1) The drug has less potential for abuse than the drugs in schedules I and II, (2) the drug has a currently accepted medical use in treatment in the United States, and (3) abuse of the drug may lead to moderate or low physical dependence or high psychological dependence. Anabolic "body building" steroids, ketamine, and many barbiturates are examples of Schedule III substances.

Schedule IV—(1) The drug has a low potential for abuse relative to the drugs in Schedule III, (2) the drug has a currently accepted medical use in treatment in the United States, and (3) abuse of the drug may lead to limited physical dependence or psychological dependence relative to the drugs or other substances in Schedule III. Antianxiety drugs such as Valium and Xanax, as well as prescription sleeping pills such as Ambien and Lunesta are examples of Schedule IV substances.

Schedule V—(1) The drug has a low potential for abuse relative to the drugs or other substances in Schedule IV, (2) the drug has a currently accepted medical use in treatment in the United States, and (3) abuse of the drug may lead to limited physical dependence or psychological dependence relative to the drugs or other substances in Schedule IV. Certain narcotic-containing prescription cough medicines such as Motofen, Lomotil and Kapectolin PG are classified as Schedule V substances.

Notes

Chapter 1

1. D. E. Nichols, "Differences between the Mechanism of Action of MDMA, MBDB, and the Classic Hallucinogens: Identification of a New Therapeutic Class: Entactogens," *Journal of Psychoactive Drugs* 18, 4 (1986): 305–13.
2. R. S. El-Mallakh and H. D. Abraham, "MDMA (Ecstasy)." *Annals of Clinical Psychiatry* 19, no. 1 (2007): 45-52; P. M. Gahlinger, *Illegal Drugs: A Complete Guide to their History, Chemistry, Use and Abuse,* Salt Lake City: Sagebrush Press, 2001.
3. P. M. Gahlinger, *Illegal Drugs: A Complete Guide to their History, Chemistry, Use and Abuse,* Salt Lake City: Sagebrush Press, 2001; A. C. Parrott, "Is Ecstasy MDMA? A Review of the Proportion of Ecstasy Tablets Containing MDMA, Their Dosage Levels, and the Changing Perceptions of Purity," *Psychopharmacology* 173, 3–4 (2004): 234–41.
4. G. N. Hayner, "MDMA Misrepresentation: An Unresolved Problem for Ecstasy Users," *Journal of Psychoactive Drugs* 34, no. 2 (2002): 195–8; A. C. Parrott, "Is Ecstasy MDMA? A Review of the Proportion of Ecstasy Tablets Containing MDMA, Their Dosage Levels, and the Changing Perceptions of Purity," *Psychopharmacology* 173, 3–4 (2004): 234–41.
5. T. L. Martin, "Three Cases of Fatal Paramethoxyamphetamine Overdose," *Journal of Analytical Toxicology* 25, 7 (2001): 649–51.
6. M. Duterte, C. Jacinto, P. Sales, and S. Murphy, "What's in a Label? Ecstasy Sellers' Perceptions of Pill Brands. *Journal of Psychoactive Drugs* 41, 1 (2009): 27–37.
7. Ibid.
8. Substance Abuse and Mental Health Services Administration (SAMHSA), *The National Survey on Drug Use and Health (NSDUH) Report,* "Use of Specific Hallucinogens:

2006" (Rockville, Md.: Office of Applied Studies, 2006); SAMHSA, *Results from the 2001 National Household Survey on Drug Abuse: Volume I. Summary of National Findings* (Rockville, Md.: Office of Applied Studies, 2002); J. C. Maxwell, "Party Drugs: Properties, Prevalence, Patterns, and Problems," *Substance Use and Misuse* 40, 9–10 (2005): 1203–40.

9. SAMHSA, *Results from the 2001 National Household Survey on Drug Abuse: Volume I. Summary of National Findings* (Rockville, Md.: Office of Applied Studies, 2002).

10. K. Suy, F. Gijsenbergh, and L. Baute, "Emergency Medical Assistance during a Mass Gathering. *European Journal of Emergency Medicine* 6, 3 (1999): 249–54.

Chapter 2

1. A. T. Shulgin and D. E. Nichols, "Characterization of Three New Psychotomimetics," in *The Psychopharmacology of Hallucinogens* (New York: Pergamon Press, 1978), 74–83.

2. D. Bennet, "Dr. Ecstasy," *New York Times Magazine*, January 30, 2005, http://www.nytimes.com/2005/01/30/magazine/30ECSTASY.html?_r=1 (accessed February 3, 2010).

3. R. W. Freudenmann, F. Oxler, and S. Bernschneider-Reif, "The Origin of MDMA (Ecstasy) Revisited: The True Story Reconstructed from the Original Documents," *Addiction* 101, 9 (2006): 1241-5; S. Bernschneider-Reif, F. Oxler, and R.W. Freudenmann, "The Origin of MDMA ("Ecstasy")— Separating the Facts from the Myth," *Pharmazie* 61, 11 (2006): 966–72

4. A. R. Pentney, "An Exploration of the History and Controversies surrounding MDMA and MDA," *Journal of Psychoactive Drugs* 33, 3 (2001): 213–21.

5. H. F. Hardman, C. O. Haavik, and M. H. Seevers, "Relationship of the Structure of Mescaline and Seven Analogs to Toxicity and Behavior in Five Species of Laboratory Animals," *Toxicology and Applied Pharmacology* 25, 2 (1973): 299–309.

6. S. Biniecki and E. Krajewski, "Production of d,1-N-methyl-beta-(3,4-methylenedioxyphenyl)-isopropylamine and d,1-N-methyl-beta-(3,4-dimethoxyphenyl)-isopropylamine," *Acta Poloniae*

Pharmaceutica 17 (1960): 421–5.

7. G. R. Greer and R. Tolbert, "The Therapeutic Use of MDMA," in *Ecstasy: The Clinical, Pharmacological, and Neurotoxicological Effects of the Drug MDMA*, ed. S. J. Peroutka (Boston: Kluwer Academic, 1990).

8. A. T. Shulgin, "History of MDMA," in *Ecstasy: The Clinical, Pharmacological, and Neurotoxicological Effects of the Drug MDMA*, ed. S. J. Peroutka (Boston: Kluwer Academic, 1990).

9. See note 4 above.

10. See note 1 above.

11. See note 7 above.

12. A. Shulgin and A. Shulgin, *Phenethylamines I Have Known and Loved: A Chemical Love Story (PIHKAL)* (Berkeley, Calf.: Transform Press, 1991).

13. A. T. Shulgin, "Psychotomimetic Drugs: Structure-activity Relationships," in *Handbook of Psychopharmacology*, eds. L. L. Iverson, S. D. Iversen, and S. H. Snyder (New York: Plenum Press, 1978).

14. J. A. Gunn, M. R. Gurd, and I. Sachs, "The Action of Some Amines Related to Adrenaline: Methyoxyphenylisopropylamines," *Journal of Physiology* 95, (1939): 485–500.

15. Loman, J., P.G. Myerson and A. Myerson, "Experimental Pharmacology of Post-encephalitic Parkinson's Disease," *Transactions of the American Neurological Association* 67 (1941): 201–3.

16. See note 12.

17. See note 13.

18. C. Naranjo, A. T. Shulgin, and T. Sargent, "Evaluation of 3,4-methylenedioxyamphetamine (MDA) as an Adjunct to Psychotherapy," *Medical Pharmacology Experimental* 17, 4 (1967): 359–64.

19. T. R. Gaston and G.T. Rasmussen, "Identification of 3,4-methylenedioxymethamphetamine," *Microgram* 5 (1972): 60–3.

20. See note 4.

21. J. Beck and M. Rosenbaum, *The Pursuit of Ecstasy: The MDMA Experience* (New York: State University of New York Press, 1994).

22. A. T. Shulgin, "The Background and Chemistry of MDMA," *Journal of Psychoactive Drugs* 18, 4 (1986): 291–304.

23. See note 8.

24. Ibid.

25. S. J. Peroutka, "Recreational Use of MDMA," in *Ecstasy: The Clinical, Pharmacological, and Neurotoxicological Effects of the Drug MDMA*, ed. S. J. Peroutka

(Boston: Kluwer Academic, 1990).

26. M. Rosenbaum, "Ecstasy: America's New "Reefer Madness," *Journal of Psychoactive Drugs* 34, 2 (2002): 137–42.

Chapter 3

1. J. A. Rochester and J. T. Kirchner, "Ecstasy (3,4-methylenedioxymethamphetamine): History, Neurochemistry, and Toxicology," *Journal of the American Board of Family Practice* 12, 2 (1999): 137–42.

2. G. A. Gudelsky and B.K. Yamamoto, "Actions of 3,4-methylenedioxymethamphetamine (MDMA) on Cerebral Dopaminergic, Serotonergic and Cholinergic Neurons," *Pharmacology, Biochemistry, and Behavvior* 90, 2 (2008): 198–207; J. Morton, "Ecstasy: Pharmacology and Neurotoxicity," *Current Opinion in Pharmacology* 5, 1 (2005): 79–86; A. R. Green et al., "The Pharmacology and Clinical Pharmacology of 3,4-methylenedioxymethamphetamine (MDMA, "Ecstasy")," *Pharmacological Reviews* 55, 3 (2003): 463–508.

3. A. R. Green et al., "The Pharmacology and Clinical Pharmacology of 3,4-methyl-enedioxymethamphetamine (MDMA, "Ecstasy")," *Pharmacological Reviews* 55, 3 (2003): 463–508; R. de la Torre et al., "Human Pharmacology of MDMA: Pharmacokinetics, Metabolism, and Disposition," *Therapeutic Drug Monitoring* 26, 2 (2004): 137–44; H. Kalant, "The Pharmacology and Toxicology of "Ecstasy" (MDMA) and Related Drugs," *Canadian Medical Association Journal* 165, 7 (2001): 917–28; D. S. Harris et al., "Subjective and Hormonal Effects of 3,4-methylenedioxymethamphetamine (MDMA) in Humans," *Psychopharmacology (Berl)* 162, 4 (2002): 396–405.

4. A. R. Green et al., "The Pharmacology and Clinical Pharmacology of 3,4-methyl-enedioxymethamphetamine (MDMA, "Ecstasy")," *Pharmacological Reviews* 55, 3 (2003): 463–508; R. de la Torre et al., "Human Pharmacology of MDMA: Pharmacokinetics, Metabolism, and Disposition," *Therapeutic Drug Monitoring* 26, 2 (2004): 137–44.

5. C. A. Baylen and H. Rosenberg, "A Review of the Acute Subjective Effects of MDMA/Ecstasy," *Addiction* 101, 7 (2006): 933–47; J. C. Cole and H. R. Sumnall, "Altered

States: The Clinical Effects of Ecstasy," *Pharmacology & Therapeutics* 98, 1 (2003): 35–58; R. S. Cohen, *The Love Drug: Marching to the Beat of Ecstasy* (New York: Haworth Medical Press, 1998).

6. R. S. Cohen, *The Love Drug: Marching to the Beat of Ecstasy* (New York: Haworth Medical Press, 1998); F. X. Vollenweider et al., "Psychological and Cardiovascular Effects and Short-term Sequelae of MDMA ("Ecstasy") in MDMA-naive Healthy Volunteers," *Neuropsychopharmacology* 19, 4 (1998): 241–51.

7. K. McElrath and K. McEvoy, "Negative Experiences on Ecstasy: The Role of Drug, Set and Setting," *Journal of Psychoactive Drugs* 34, 2 (2002): 199–208.

8. M. E. Liechti, A. Gamma, and F. X. Vollenweider, "Gender Differences in the Subjective Effects of MDMA," *Psychopharmacology (Berl)* 154, 2 (2001): 161–8.

9. K. Allott and J. Redman, "Are There Sex Differences Associated with the Effects of Ecstasy/3,4-methylenedioxymethamphetamine (MDMA)?" *Neuroscience & Biobehavoral Reviews* 31, 3 (2007): 327–47.

10. H. Kalant, "The Pharmacology and Toxicology of "Ecstasy" (MDMA) and Related Drugs," *Canadian Medical Association Journal* 165, 7 (2001): 917–28; L. R. Gowing, "The Health Effects of Ecstasy: A Literature Review," *Drug and Alcohol Review* 21 (2002): 53–63.

11. H. S. Brand et al., "Ecstasy (MDMA) and Oral Health," *British Dental Journal* 204, 2 (2008): 77–81.

12. H. Kalant, "The Pharmacology and Toxicology of "Ecstasy" (MDMA) and Related Drugs," *Canadian Medical Association Journal* 165, 7 (2001): 917–28; L. R. Gowing et al., "The Health Effects of Ecstasy: A Literature Review," *Drug and Alcohol Review* 21, (2002): 53–63; A. P. Hall and J. A. Henry, "Acute Toxic Effects of 'Ecstasy' (MDMA) and Related Compounds: Overview of Pathophysiology and Clinical Management," *British Journal of Anaesthesia* 96, 6 (2006): 678–85.

13. L. R. Gowing et al., "The Health Effects of Ecstasy: A Literature Review," *Drug and Alcohol Review* 21, (2002): 53–63; J. A. Henry et al., "Toxicity and Deaths from 3,4-methylenedioxymethamphetamine ('Ecstasy')," *Lancet*

340, 8816 (1992): 384–7; B. O'Connor, "Hazards Associated with the Recreational Drug 'Ecstasy,' *British Journal of Hospital Medicine* 52, 10 (1994): 507, 510–514; F. Schifano, "A Bitter Pill: Overview of Ecstasy (MDMA, MDA) Related Fatalities," *Psychopharmacology (Berl)* 173, 3–4 (2004): 242-8; F. Schifano et al., "Death Rates from Ecstasy (MDMA, MDA) and Polydrug Use in England and Wales 1996–2002," *Human Psychopharmacology* 18, 7 (2003): 519–24.

14. A. R. Green, E. O'Shea, and M.I. Colado, "A Review of the Mechanisms Involved in the Acute MDMA (Ecstasy)-induced Hyperthermic Response," *European Journal of Pharmacology* 500, 1–3 (2004): 3–13

15. G. A. Campbell and M. H. Rosner, "The Agony of Ecstasy: MDMA (3,4-methylene-dioxymethamphetamine) and the Kidney," *Clinical Journal of the American Society of Nephrology* 3, 6 (2008): 1852–60.

16. Ibid.

17. J. C. Cole and H. R. Sumnall, "Altered States: The Clinical Effects of Ecstasy," *Pharmacology & Therapeutics* 98, 1 (2003): 35–58; A. P. Hall and J. A. Henry, "Acute Toxic Effects of 'Ecstasy' (MDMA) and Related Compounds: Overview of Pathophysiology and Clinical Management," *British Journal of Anaesthesia* 96, 6 (2006): 678–85; E. Silins, J. Copeland, and P. Dillon, "Qualitative Review of Serotonin Syndrome, Ecstasy (MDMA), and the Use of Other Serotonergic Substances: Hierarchy of Risk," *Australian and New Zealand Journal of Psychiatry* 41, 8 (2007): 649–55; A. C. Parrott, "Recreational Ecstasy/MDMA, the Serotonin Syndrome, and Serotonergic Neurotoxicity," *Pharmacology, Biochemistry, and Behavior* 71, 4 (2002): 837–44.

18. A. R. Green et al., "The Pharmacology and Clinical Pharmacology of 3,4-methylenedioxymethamphetamine (MDMA, "Ecstasy"), *Pharmacological Reviews* 55, 3 (2003): 463–508.

19. J. C. Cole and H. R. Sumnall, "Altered States: The Clinical Effects of Ecstasy," *Pharmacology & Therapeutics* 98, 1 (2003): 35–58; L. R. Gowing et al., "The Health Effects of Ecstasy: A Literature Review," *Drug and Alcohol Review* 21, (2002): 53–63.

20. U. D. McCann and G. A. Ricaurte, "Effects of (+/-) 3,4-methylenedioxymethamphetamine (MDMA) on Sleep and Circadian Rhythms," *ScientificWorldJournal* 7, (2007): 231-8; T. Schierenbeck et al., "Effect of Illicit Recreational Drugs upon Sleep: Cocaine, Ecstasy and Marijuana," *Sleep Medicine Review* 12, 5 (2008): 381–9.

21. H. Kalant, "The Pharmacology and Toxicology of "Ecstasy" (MDMA) and Related Drugs," *Canadian Medical Association Journal* 165, 7 (2001): 917–28; A. P. Hall and J. A. Henry, "Acute Toxic Effects of 'Ecstasy' (MDMA) and Related Compounds: Overview of Pathophysiology and Clinical Management," *British Journal of Anaesthesia* 96, 6 (2006): 678–85.

22. S. F. Marasco and H. K. Lim, "Ecstasy-associated Pneumomediastinum," *Annals of the Royal College of Surgeons of England* 89, 4 (2007): 389–93.

23. A. Sharma, "A Case of Sensorineural Deafness Following Ingestion of Ecstasy," *Journal of Laryngology and Otology* 115, 11 (2001): 911–15.

24. S. Kaye, S. Darke, and J. Duflou, "Methylenedioxymethamphetamine (MDMA)-related Fatalities in Australia: Demographics, Circumstances, Toxicology and Major Organ Pathology," *Drug and Alcohol Dependence* 104, 3 (2009): 254–61; S. M. Gore, "Fatal Uncertainty: Death-rate from Use of Ecstasy or Heroin," *Lancet* 354, 9186 (1999): 1265–6.

25. S. Kaye, S. Darke, and J. Duflou, "Methylenedioxymethamphetamine (MDMA)-related Fatalities in Australia: Demographics, Circumstances, Toxicology and Major Organ Pathology," *Drug and Alcohol Dependence* 104, 3 (2009): 254–61.

26. K. J. Clemens, "Repeated Weekly Exposure to MDMA, Methamphetamine or Their Combination: Long-term Behavioural and Neurochemical Effects in Rats," *Drug and Alcohol Dependence* 86, 2-3 (2007): 183–90; A. C. Parrott et al., "Cannabis and Ecstasy/MDMA (3,4-methylenedioxymethamphetamine): An Analysis of their Neuropsychobiological Interactions in Recreational Users," *Journal Neural Transmission* 114, 8 (2007): 959–68; E. Gouzoulis-Mayfrank and J. Daumann, "The Confounding Problem of Polydrug Use in Recreational Ecstasy/MDMA Users: A Brief

Overview," *Journal of Psychopharmacology* 20, 2 (2006): 188-93; L. Topp et al., "Ecstasy Use in Australia: Patterns of Use and Associated Harm," *Drug and Alcohol Dependence* 55, 1–2 (1999): 105–15.

27. H. Kalant, "The Pharmacology and Toxicology of "Ecstasy" (MDMA) and Related Drugs," *Canadian Medical Association Journal* 165, 7 (2001): 917–28; S. N. Karlsen, O. Spigset, and L. Slordal, "The Dark Side of Ecstasy: Neuropsychiatric Symptoms After Exposure to 3,4-methylenedioxymethamphetamine," *Basic & Clinical Pharmacology & Toxicology* 102, 1 (2008): 15–24; A. C. Parrott, "Human Psychopharmacology of Ecstasy (MDMA): A Review of 15 Years of Empirical Research," *Human Psychopharmacology: Clinical and Experimental* 16, 8 (2001): 557–577; K. K. Zakzanis, Z. Campbell, and D. Jovanovski, "The Neuropsychology of Ecstasy (MDMA) Use: A Quantitative Review," *Human Psychopharmacology* 22, 7 (2007): 427–35; R. Thomasius et al., "Mental Disorders in Current and Former Heavy Ecstasy (MDMA) Users," *Addiction* 100, 9 (2005): 1310-9; K. L. Hanson and

M. Luciana, "Neurocognitive Function in Users of MDMA: The Importance of Clinically Significant Patterns of Use," *Psychological Medicine* 34, 2 (2004): 229–46.

28. H. Kalant, "The Pharmacology and Toxicology of "Ecstasy" (MDMA) and Related Drugs. *Canadian Medical Association Journal* 165, 7 (2001): 917–28; S. N. Karlsen, O. Spigset, and L. Slordal, "The Dark Side of Ecstasy: Neuropsychiatric Symptoms After Exposure to 3,4-methylenedioxymethamphetamine," *Basic & Clinical Pharmacology & Toxicology* 102, 1 (2008): 15–24; A. C. Parrott, "Human Psychopharmacology of Ecstasy (MDMA): A Review of 15 Years of Empirical Research," *Human Psychopharmacology: Clinical and Experimental* 16, 8 (2001): 557–577; K. K. Zakzanis, Z. Campbell and D. Jovanovski, "The Neuropsychology of Ecstasy (MDMA) Use: A Quantitative Review," *Human Psychopharmacology* 22, 7 (2007): 427–35; C. Guillot, "Is Recreational Ecstasy (MDMA) Use Associated with Higher Levels of Depressive Symptoms?" *Journal of Psychoactive Drugs* 39, 1 (2007): 31–9; L. T. Wu et al., "Hallucinogen-related

Disorders in a National Sample of Adolescents: The Influence of Ecstasy/MDMA Use," *Drug and Alcohol Dependence* 104, 1–2 (2009): 156–66; M. A. Landabaso et al., "Ecstasy-induced Psychotic Disorder: Six-month Follow-up Study," *European Addiction Research* 8, 3 (2002): 133–40.

29. K. Soar, A. C. Parrott, and H. C. Fox, "Persistent Neuropsychological Problems After 7 years of Abstinence from Recreational Ecstasy (MDMA): A Case Study," *Psychological Reports* 95, 1 (2004): 192–6; E. Gouzoulis-Mayfrank, et al., "Memory Performance in Polyvalent MDMA (Ecstasy) Users Who Continue or Discontinue MDMA Use," *Drug and Alcohol Dependence* 78, 3 (2005): 317–23; E. Gouzoulis-Mayfrank and J. Daumann, "Neurotoxicity of Methylene-dioxyamphetamines (MDMA; Ecstasy) in Humans: How Strong Is the Evidence for Persistent Brain Damage?" *Addiction* 101, 3 (2006): 348–61.

30. H. Kalant, "The Pharmacology and Toxicology of "Ecstasy" (MDMA) and Related Drugs," *Canadian Medical Association Journal* 165, 7 (2001): 917–28.

31. A. C. Parrott, "Chronic Rolerance to Recreational MDMA (3,4-methylenedioxymetham-phetamine) or Ecstasy," *Journal of Psychopharmacology* 19, 1 (2005): 71–83.

32. H. Kalant, "The Pharmacology and Toxicology of "Ecstasy" (MDMA) and Related Drugs," *Canadian Medical Association Journal* 165, 7 (2001): 917–28; M. S. Quinton and B. K. Yamamoto, "Causes and Consequences of Methamphetamine and MDMA Toxicity," *American Association of Pharmaceutical Scientists Journal* 8, 2 (2006): E337–47.

33. F. Bai et al., "Serotonergic Neurotoxicity of 3,4-(+/-)-methylenedioxyamphetamine and 3,4-(+/-)-methylen-dioxymethamphetamine (ecstasy) Is Potentiated by Inhibition of Gamma-glutamyl Transpeptidase," *Chemical Research in Toxicology* 14, 7 (2001): 863–70; F. Bai, S. S. Lau, and T. J. Monks, "Glutathione and N-acetylcysteine Conjugates of Alpha-methyldopamine Produce Serotonergic Neurotoxicity: Possible Role in Methylenedioxyamphetamine-mediated Neurotoxicity," *Chemical Research in Toxicology* 12, 12 (1999): 1150–7; T. J. Monks, F. Bai, R. T. Miller and S. S. Lau, Serotonergic Neurotoxicity of Methylene-

dioxyamphetamine and Methylenedioxymetamphetamine," *Advances in Experimental Medicine and Biology* 500 (2001): 397–406; T. J. Monks et al., "The Role of Metabolism in 3,4-(+)-methylenedioxyamphetamine and 3,4-(+)-methylenedioxymethamphetamine (Ecstasy) Toxicity," *Therapeutic Drug Monitoring* 26, 2 (2004): 132–6.

34. J. Morton, "Ecstasy: Pharmacology and Neurotoxicity," *Current Opinion in Pharmacology* 5, 1 (2005): 79–86; R. L. Cowan, "Neuroimaging Research in Human MDMA Users: A Review," *Psychopharmacology (Berl)* 189, 4 (2007): 539–56.

35. J. Morton, "Ecstasy: Pharmacology and Neurotoxicity," *Current Opinion in Pharmacology* 5, 1 (2005): 79–86; R. L. Cowan, "Neuroimaging Research in Human MDMA Users: A Review," *Psychopharmacology (Berl)* 189, 4 (2007): 539–56; U. D. McCann et al., "Positron Emission Tomographic Evidence of Toxic Effect of MDMA ("Ecstasy") on Brain Serotonin Neurons in Human Beings," *Lancet* 352, 9138 (1998): 1433–7.

36. U. D. McCann, V. Eligulashvili, and G. A. Ricaurte, "(+/-)3,4-Methylenedioxymethamphetamine ('Ecstasy')-induced Serotonin Neurotoxicity: Clinical Studies," *Neuropsychobiology* 42, 1 (2000): 11–6.

37. R. Buchert et al., "Reversibility of Ecstasy-induced Reduction in Serotonin Rransporter Availability in Polydrug Ecstasy Users," *European Journal of Nuclear Medicine and Molecular Imaging*," 33, no. 2 (2006): 188–99.

Chapter 4

1. A. T. Shulgin, "The Background and Chemistry of MDMA," *Journal of Psychoactive Drugs* 18, 4 (1986): 291–304.

2. K. L. Jansen, "Ecstasy (MDMA) Dependence," *Drug and Alcohol Dependence* 53, 2 (1999): 121–24; A. T. Shulgin, "The Background and Chemistry of MDMA," *Journal of Psychoactive Drugs* 18, 4 (1986): 291–304; H. Kalant, "The Pharmacology and Toxicology of "Ecstasy" (MDMA) and Related Drugs," *Canadian Medical Association Journal* 165, 7 (2001): 917–28.

3. G. J. Peters, G. Kok, and H. P. Schaalma, "Careers in Ecstasy Use: Do Ecstasy Users Cease of Their Own Accord? Implications for Intervention Development," *Bio Med Central Public*

Health 8 (2008): 376; H. K. Ver-
vaeke, L. van Deursen, and
D. J. Korf, "The Role of Peers
in the Initiation and Continua-
tion of Ecstasy Use," *Substance
Use & Misuse* 43, no. 5 (2008):
633–46; S. S. Martins et al.,
"Adolescent Ecstasy and Other
Drug Use in the National
Survey of Parents and Youth:
The Role of Sensation-seeking,
Parental Monitoring and Peer's
Drug Use," *Addictive Behav-
iors* 33, no. 7 (2008): 919–33;
C. F. Yen et al., "Family, Peer
and Individual Factors Related
to Methylenedioxymetham-
phetamine Use in Taiwanese
Adolescents," *Psychiatry and
Clinical Neuroscience* 61, no. 5
(2007): 552–57.

4. G. J. Peters, G. Kok, and H.P.
Schaalma, "Careers in Ecstasy
Use: Do Ecstasy Users Cease of
Their Own Accord? Implica-
tions for Intervention Develop-
ment," *BMC Public Health* 8
(2008): 376; H. K. Vervaeke,
L. van Deursen, and D. J.
Korf, "The Role of Peers in the
Initiation and Continuation
of Ecstasy Use," *SubstanceUse
& Misuse* 43, no. 5 (2008):
633–46; M. J. Baggott, "Pre-
venting Problems in Ecstasy
Users: Reduce Use to Reduce
Harm," *Journal of Psychoactive
Drugs* 34, 2 (2002): 145–62.

5. G. J. Peters, G. Kok, and H. P.
Schaalma, "Careers in Ecstasy
Use: Do Ecstasy Users Cease of
Their Own Accord? Implica-
tions for Intervention Develop-
ment," *Bio Med Central Public
Health* 8 (2008): 376.

6. American Psychiatric Associa-
tion, *Diagnostic and Statistical
Manual of Mental Disorders,
4th Edition, Text Revision.*
(Washington, DC: American
Psychiatric Press, 2004).

7. L. B. Cottler et al., "Ecstasy
Abuse and Dependence
Among Adolescents and Young
Adults: Applicability and Reli-
ability of DSM-IV Criteria,"
Human Psychopharmacology
16, 8 (2001): 599–606.

8. L. B. Cottler, K. S. Leung, and
A. B. Abdallah, "Test-re-test
Reliability of DSM-IV Adopted
Criteria for 3,4-methylene-
dioxymethamphetamine
(MDMA) Abuse and Depen-
dence: A Cross-national Study."
Addiction (2009); L. M. Scheier
et al., "Tri-city Study of Ecstasy
Use Problems: A Latent Class
Analysis," *Drug and Alcohol
Dependence* 98, 3 (2008):
249–63.

9. C. F. Yen and S.Y. Hsu, "Symptoms of Ecstasy Dependence
and Correlation with Psycho-
pathology in Taiwanese Adolescents," *Journal of Nervous*

and Mental Disease 195, 10
(2007): 866–69.

10. A. L. Stone et al., "Who Is
Becoming Hallucinogen
Dependent Soon After Hallu-
cinogen Use Starts?" *Drug and
Alcohol Dependence* 87, 2–3
(2007): 153–63; A. L. Stone,
C. L. Storr, and J. C. Anthony,
"Evidence for a Hallucino-
gen Dependence Syndrome
Developing Soon After Onset
of Hallucinogen Use During
Adolescence," *Internaltional
Journal of Methods in Psychi-
atric Research* 15, 3 (2006):
116–30.

11. L. T. Wu et al., "Hallucinogen-
related Disorders in a National
Sample of Adolescents: The
Influence of Ecstasy/MDMA
Use," *Drug and Alcohol Depen-
dence* 104, 1–2 (2009): 156–66.

12. R. Thomasius, "Mental Disorders in Current and Former
Heavy Ecstasy (MDMA)
Users," *Addiction* 100, 9 (2005):
1310–9.

13. R. Thomasius et al., "Mental
Disorders in Current and For-
mer Heavy Ecstasy (MDMA)
Users," *Addiction* 100, 9 (2005):
1310–9; K. L. Hanson and
M. Luciana, "Neurocognitive
Function in Users of MDMA:
The Importance of Clinically
Significant Patterns of Use."
Psychological Medicine 34, no. 2
(2004): 229–46.

14. L. T. Wu et al., "Hallucinogen-
related Disorders in a National
Sample of Adolescents: The
Influence of Ecstasy/MDMA
Use," Drug and Alcohol Depen-
dence 104, 1–2 (2009): 156–66;
L. T. Wu, W. E. Schlenger, and
D. M. Galvin, "Concurrent
Use of Methamphetamine,
MDMA, LSD, Ketamine, GHB,
and Flunitrazepam among
American Youths," Drug and
Alcohol Dependence 84, 1
(2006): 102–13; S. S. Martins,
L. A. Ghandour, and H. D.
Chilcoat, "Pathways between
Ecstasy Initiation and Other
Drug Use," Addictive Behav-
iors 32, 7 (2007): 1511–18;
S. S. Martins, G. Mazzotti,
and H. D. Chilcoat, "Recent-
onset Ecstasy Use: Associa-
tion with Deviant Behaviors
and Psychiatric Comorbidity,"
Experimental and Clinical Psy-
chopharmacology 14, 3 (2006):
275–86; K. Soar, A. Parrott,
and J. Turner, "Attributions
for Psychobiological Changes
in Ecstasy/MDMA and Other
Polydrug Users," Journal of
Psychopharmacology 23, 7
(2009): 745–58; L. W. Reid,
K. W. Elifson and C. E. Sterk,
"Ecstasy and Gateway Drugs:
Initiating the Use of Ecstasy
and Other Drugs," Annals of
Epidemiology 17, 1 (2007):
74–80; P. Zimmermann et al.,

"Pathways into Ecstasy Use: The Role of Prior Cannabis Use and Ecstasy Availability," Drug and Alcohol Dependence 79, no. 3 (2005): 331–41.

Chapter 5

1. K. L. Jansen, "Ecstasy (MDMA) Dependence," Drug and Alcohol Dependence 53, 2 (1999): 121–24.
2. S. C. Koesters, P. D. Rogers, and C. R. Rajasingham, "MDMA ('Ecstasy') and Other 'Club Drugs:' The New Epidemic," *Pediatric Clinics of North America* 49, no. 2 (2002): 415–33.
3. Ibid.
4. G. N. Hayner, "MDMA Misrepresentation: An Unresolved Problem for Ecstasy Users," *Journal of Psychoactive Drugs* 34, 2 (2002): 195–98.
5. G. J. Peters, G. Kok, and C. Abraham, "Social Cognitive Determinants of Ecstasy Use to Target in Evidence-based Interventions: A Meta-analytical Review," *Addiction* 103, 1 (2008): 109–18.

Chapter 6

1. R. Doblin, "A Clinical Plan for MDMA (Ecstasy) in the Treatment of Posttraumatic Stress Disorder (PTSD): Partnering with the FDA," *Journal of Psychoactive Drugs* 34, 2 (2002): 185–94.

2. R. Doblin, "A Clinical Plan for MDMA (Ecstasy) in the Treatment of Posttraumatic Stress Disorder (PTSD)," *Journal of Psychoactive Drugs* 34, 2 (2002): 185–94; A. C. Parrott, "The Psychotherapeutic Potential of MDMA (3,4-methylenedioxymethamphetamine): An Evidence-based Review," Psychopharmacology (Berl) 191, 2 (2007): 181–93; P. O. Johansen and T. S. Krebs, "How Could MDMA (Ecstasy) Help Anxiety Disorders? A Neurobiological Rationale," Journal of Psychopharmacology 23, 4 (2009): 389–91.
3. K. L. Jansen and L. Theron, "Ecstasy (MDMA), Methamphetamine, and Date Rape (Drug-facilitated Sexual Assault): A Consideration of the Issues," *Journal of Psychoactive Drugs* 38, 1 (2006): 1–12.
4. A. C. Parrott, "The Psychotherapeutic Potential of MDMA (3,4-methylenedioxymethamphetamine): An Evidence-based Review," *Psychopharmacology (Berl)* 191, 2 (2007): 181–93
5. M. E. Liechti, A. Gamma, and F. X. Vollenweider, "Gender Differences in the Subjective Effects of MDMA," *Psychopharmacology (Berl)* 154, 2 (2001): 161–8.

6. R. Metzner and S. Adamson, "Using MDMA in Healing, Psychotherapy and Spiritual Practice," in *Ecstasy: The Complete Guide*, ed. J. Holland, J. (Rochester, NY: Park Street Press, 2001).

7. R. Doblin, "A Clinical Plan for MDMA (Ecstasy) in the Treatment of Posttraumatic Stress Disorder (PTSD)," *Journal of Psychoactive Drugs* 34, 2 (2002): 185–94; G. Greer and R. Tolbert, "Subjective Reports of the Effects of MDMA in a Clinical Setting," *Journal of Psychoactive Drugs* 18, 4 (1986): 319–27.

8. See note 4.

Glossary

active metabolite   A molecule created by the metabolic breakdown of drug or chemical substance that has significant biological activity.

acute MDMA toxicity   A state caused by excessive Ecstasy intake that has severe health consequences including dehydration and dangerous increases in body temperature.

axon   Wire-like fibers of nerve cells that transmit electrical information.

bruxism   Grinding of the teeth.

cardiac arrhythmia   Irregular heart beat.

cell body   The main compartment of a nerve cell that contains genetic material (DNA) as well as cellular machinery for making proteins.

cerebral edema   Swelling of the brain.

club drug   Typically refers to Ecstasy, gamma-hydroxybutyrate (GHB), or other intoxicating drugs that are frequently used by patrons of nighttime dance clubs.

coagulation   Thickening of the blood.

cognitive-behavioral therapy (CBT)   A series of strategies aimed at correcting negative thought patterns and emotional responses in order to treat a psychological disorder such as depression.

date rape drug   A drug that is given unknowingly to a person that renders him or her too sedated to defend his or herself from unwanted sexual advances and sexual assault.

dehydration   Significant loss of water content of the body.

dendrite   Branched fibers of nerve cells that receive information from other nerve cells.

depersonalization   A feeling that one's body or surroundings are detached or not real, or viewing oneself from outside his or her own body (i.e., an "out-of-body" experience).

diaphoresis   Excessive sweating.

diuretic   A substance that decreases water retention by the kidneys and results in excessive urination.

emesis   Vomiting.

empathogen   A chemical or drug that increases feelings of empathy.

empathogenesis   The process of increasing feelings of empathy.

empathy   The ability to experience and understand the emotions and feelings of other people.

entactogen   A chemical or drug that increases positive feelings about oneself and the world in which he or she lives.

entactogenesis   The process of increasing positive feelings about oneself and the world in which he or she lives.

ephedrine   A nervous system stimulant.

euphoria   A state of extreme pleasure, exhilaration, and sense of well-being.

flashback   A sudden, realistic, and often frightening reliving of a memory.

flunitrazepam   A potent sedative drug often used in committing date rape.

gamma-hydroxybutyrate (GHB)   A potent intoxicating drug that is often used in committing date rape.

gateway theory   The theory that use of some drugs, such as marijuana or Ecstasy, leads to subsequent use of "harder" drugs such as cocaine, heroin, or methamphetamine.

half-life   The time required for the body to metabolize or excrete half of a given amount of drug or other chemical substance.

hallucination   A distorted perception of one or more of the five senses (touch, taste, smell, vision, or hearing) or a perception of something that does not actually exist.

hallucinogen   A chemical or drug that produces hallucinations.

harm reduction   Strategies aimed at counteracting some of the negative physiological effects of Ecstasy, including drinking lots of water prior to taking Ecstasy to prevent dehydration, or testing the purity of Ecstasy pills.

hemophilia   A bleeding disorder characterized by a decreased ability to form clots and heal wounds.

hemorrhage   Internal bleeding due to rupture of a blood vessel.

hemorrhagic stroke   A loss of oxygen to the brain due to the rupture of a blood vessel.

hepatitis   Inflammation, infection, or abnormal functioning of the liver.

herbal Ecstasy   Extracts of the Ephedra plant that produces effects similar to those produced by Ecstasy.

hyperprexia   Body temperature that is increased above the normal range; also called hyperthermia.

hypertension   Blood pressure that is increased above the normal range.

hyperthermia   Body temperature that is increased above the normal range; also called hyperprexia.

hyperventilation   Rate of breathing that is increased above the normal range.

hyponatremia   An imbalance of electrolytes in the blood often caused by excessive water intake.

ischemic stroke   Loss of oxygen to the brain due to a blocked artery.

MDMA   Abbreviation for 3,4-methylenedioxymethamphetamine, the chemical name of Ecstasy.

mydriasis   Dilation of the pupils of the eye.

myoglobin   A highly abundant protein found in muscle tissue.

neuron   Nerve cell.

neurotransmitter   Chemical messenger used by nerve cells to communicate with each other

nucleus   The part of the nerve cell body that contains genetic material (DNA).

nystagmus   Irregular movement patterns of the eyes.

Parkinson's disease   A debilitating disease of the nervous system that causes symptoms such as trembling and involuntary movements of the arms, hands, or legs.

pneumomediastinum   A condition in which air escapes from the lungs and becomes trapped between the outside of the lungs and the inside wall of the chest cavity.

post-traumatic stress disorder (PTSD)   A psychological disorder brought on by experiencing or witnessing a traumatic event that is characterized by feelings of anxiety, depression, and flashbacks.

psychedelic   Term referring to either a hallucinogen or a style of artwork and colors that is influenced by hallucinogen.

psychosis   A loss of touch with reality, usually characterized by hallucinations and unfounded beliefs

raphe nuclei   A dense cluster of nerve cells in the brainstem that extend axons to numerous areas of the brain and use serotonin as their neurotransmitter.

rave   A type of large social gathering or party usually held in an empty warehouse or other large place with dancing, music, lights, and use of alcohol and drugs including Ecstasy.

receptor   A protein designed to recognize a specific neurotransmitter molecule.

relapse   Resumption of taking a drug or drugs after a period of being abstinent.

rhabdomyolysis   A breakdown of muscle tissue due to prolonged seizures or physical activity.

serotonergic neurotoxicity   Selective damage or death of nerve cells in the brain that use serotonin as a neurotransmitter.

serotonin   Also known as 5-hydroxytryptamine (5-HT), a highly abundant neurotransmitter in the brain that is involved in regulation of mood; Ecstasy causes a massive release of serotonin-containing synaptic terminals.

serotonin syndrome   A cluster of symptoms including trembling, muscle spasms, excessive sweating, aggravation, confusion, and hyperactivity; is caused by excessive release of serotonin from synaptic terminals.

sleep apnea   A condition in which a person briefly and repeatedly stops breathing during sleep due to a blockage of the airways by the tongue, soft tissue in the back of the throat, or a malfunctioning of mechanisms by which the brain controls breathing.

styptic   A chemical or drug that promotes blot clotting and healing.

substance abuse   A pattern of drug use that leads to impairments in social, occupational, or academic functioning.

substance dependence   A pattern of drug use that results in significant psychological and emotional distress, and impairment in a person's social, occupational, or academic functioning, and an inability to stop using the drug for extended periods of time.

synapse   A junction between two nerve cells where chemical messengers for communication.

synaptic terminal   The end of an axon that contains chemicals used for communicating with other nerve cells.

tachycardia   Heart rate that is increased above the normal range.

tolerance   Reduced effectiveness of a drug due to repeated drug intake, which results in increasing the amount of drug taken to achieve the same desired effects as when the drug was first used.

toxicity   The ability to cause healthy tissue or cells to become damaged or die.

transporter   A protein that transports neurotransmitter molecules back into the synaptic terminal after they have been released.

trismus   Clenching of the jaw muscles.

truth drug or truth serum   A hypothetical substance acting in the brain that would cause an individual to reveal information unwillingly.

tryptophan hydroxylase   Enzyme that is crucial for the formation of serotonin.

ulcerations   Open sores.

vesicles   Sphere-like storage compartments for neurotransmitters.

withdrawal   Unpleasant symptoms that are experienced when long-term use of a drug is suddenly stopped.

Further Resources

Books and Articles

Cole, J.C. and H.R. Sumnall, "Altered states: the clinical effects of Ecstasy." *Pharmacology and Therapeutics* 98, 1 (2003): 35–58.

El-Mallakh, R.S. and H.D. Abraham, "MDMA (Ecstasy)." *Annals of Clinical Psychiatry* 19, 1 (2007): 45–52.

Gahliger, P. *Illegal Drugs: A Complete Guide to their History, Chemistry, Use, and Abuse.* Sagebrush Publications, Tempe, AZ, 2003, 480 pp.

Green, A.R., A.O. Mechan, J.M. Elliott, E. O'Shea and M.I. Colado, "The pharmacology and clinical pharmacology of 3,4-methylenedioxymethamphetamine (MDMA, "ecstasy")." *Pharmacological Reviews* 55, 3 (2003): 463–508.

Iversen, L.. *Speed, Ecstasy, Ritalin: The Science of Amphetamines.* Oxford University Press, Oxford, UK, 2008, 222 pp.

O'Leary, G., J. Nargiso, and R.D. Weiss. "3,4-methylenedioxmethamphetamine (MDMA): a review." *Current Psychiatry Reports* 3 (2001): 477–83.

Pilcher, T. *e: The Incredibly Strange History of Ecstasy.* Running Press, Philadelphia, PA, 2008, 192 pp.

Rochester, J.A. and J.T. Kirchner, "Ecstasy (3,4-methylenedioxymethamphetamine): history, neurochemistry, and toxicology." *Journal of the American Board of Family Practice* 12, 2 (1999): 137–42.

Schroeder, B.E.. *Ecstasy.* In: Drugs: The Straight Facts (D.J. Triggle, ed), Chelsea House, Langhorn, PA, 2004, 96 pp.

Web Sites

Drug Enforcement Administration Web Site on Ecstasy
http://www.usdoj.gov/dea/concern/mdma.html

Ecstasy Information for Parents
http://www.theantidrug.com/drug_info/drug_info_ecstasy.asp

Erowid Vault on Ecstasy
http://www.erowid.org/chemicals/mdma/mdma.shtml

Facts about Ecstasy and Resources for Treatment of Ecstasy Addiction
http://www.ecstasyaddiction.com

Information on Non-Ecstasy Substances in Ecstasy Tablets
http://www.ecstasydata.org

National Institute on Drug Abuse
http://www.nida.nih.gov

Partnership for a Drug-Free America
http://www.drugfree.org

Index

About the Author

M. Foster Olive received his bachelor's degree in psychology from the University of California, San Diego, and went on to receive his Ph.D. in neuroscience from UCLA. He is currently an assistant professor in the Center for Drug and Alcohol Programs and Department of Psychiatry and Behavioral Sciences at the Medical University of South Carolina. His research focuses on the neurobiology of addiction, and he has published in numerous academic journals including *Psychopharmacology, The Journal of Neuroscience,* and *Nature Neuroscience.* He has also authored several books in the *Drugs: The Straight Facts* series, including titles such as *Peyote and Mescaline, Sleep Aids, Prescription Pain Relievers, Designer Drugs, Crack,* and *LSD.*

About the Editor

David J. Triggle is a university professor and a distinguished professor in the School of Pharmacy and Pharmaceutical Sciences at the State University of New York at Buffalo. He studied in the United Kingdom and earned a B.Sc. in chemistry from the University of Southampton and a Ph.D. in chemistry at the University of Hull. Following postdoctoral work at the University of Ottawa in Canada and the University of London in the United Kingdom, he assumed a position at the School of Pharmacy at Buffalo. He served as chairman of the Department of Biochemical Pharmacology from 1971 to 1985, and as dean of the School of Pharmacy at Buffalo from 1985 to 1995. From 1995 to 2001, he served as dean of the graduate school and as the university provost from 2000 to 2001. He is the author of several books dealing with the chemical pharmacology of the autonomic nervous system and drug-receptor interactions, some 400 scientific publications, and he has delivered more than 1,000 lectures worldwide on his research.